MW00427140

Sizzling Style

Every Word Matters

Sizzling Style: Every Word Matters
First Edition
Copyright © 2014 William Bernhardt Writing
Programs
Red Sneaker Press
An imprint of Babylon Books

ISBN: 978-0-9893789-7-0

Sizzling Style

Every Word Matters

William Bernhardt

The Red Sneaker Writer Series

The
RED SNEAKER
WRITERS BOOK SERIES

Other Books by William Bernhardt

Red Sneaker Writer Series

Story Structure: The Key to Successful Fiction
Creating Character: Bringing Your Story to Life
Perfecting Plot: Charting the Hero's Journey
Dynamic Dialogue: Letting Your Story Speak
The Fundamentals of Fiction (DVD)

The Ben Kincaid Series

Primary Justice
Blind Justice
Deadly Justice
Perfect Justice
Cruel Justice
Naked Justice
Extreme Justice
Dark Justice
Silent Justice

Murder One
Criminal Intent
Hate Crime
Death Row
Capitol Murder
Capitol Threat
Capitol Conspiracy
Capitol Offense
Capitol Betrayal

Other Novels

Nemesis: The Final Case of
Eliot Ness
Dark Eye
The Code of Buddyhood
Paladins of the Abyss
Shine

The Midnight Before
Christmas
Final Round
Double Jeopardy
Strip Search

Poetry

The White Bird

For Young Readers

Equal Justice: The Courage of Ada Lois Sipuel (biography)
Princess Alice and the Dreadful Dragon (illus. by Kerry McGhee)
The Black Sentry

Edited by William Bernhardt

Legal Briefs

Natural Suspect

Dedicated to all the Red Sneaker Writers:
You can't fail unless you quit.

The difference between the almost right word and the right word is the difference between the lightning bug and the lightning.

Mark Twain

TABLE OF CONTENTS

Introduction..i

Chapter One: Defining Style..1

Chapter Two: Grammar is Not Style.............................9

Chapter Three: The Essence of Art..............................27

Chapter Four: Clarity and Precision............................41

Chapter Five: Harnessing the Lightning......................59

Chapter Six: Spotlight on Verbs..................................77

Chapter Seven: Other Style Issues...............................91

Appendix A: Style Review..i

Appendix B: Commonly Confused Words.................iii

Appendix C: The Writer's Reading List...................xiii

INTRODUCTION

Welcome to the Red Sneaker Writers Book series. If you've read other Red Sneaker publications or attended Red Sneaker events, you can skip to Chapter One. If you're new, let me take a moment to explain.

I've been telling stories for many years, doing almost every kind of writing imaginable. I've been speaking at workshops and conferences almost as long. Every time I step behind the podium I see the same tableau staring back at me: long rows of talented people, most of whom have attended many of these events but are still frustrated by the fact that they haven't sold any books. Yes, the market is tough and agents are hard to find and self-publishing can be frustrating. But when aspiring writers do the work, put it out there, but still don't succeed...there's usually a reason. Too often enormous potential is lost due to a lack of fundamental knowledge. Sometimes a little guidance is all that stands between an unknown writer and a satisfying writing career.

The large auditorium/general information lecture is not terribly conducive to writing instruction. And sometimes the teaching I've heard offered is dubious at best. Too often speakers seem more interested in appearing "literary" than in providing useful information. Sometimes I feel presenters do more to obfuscate the subject than to explain it, that they want to make writing as mysterious and incomprehensible as possible, either because that makes them sound deeper or because they don't understand the subject themselves. How is that going to help anyone?

After giving this some thought, I formulated the Red Sneaker Writing Center. Why Red Sneakers? Because I love my red sneakers. They're practical, flexible, sturdy—and bursting with style and flair. In other words, exactly what I think writing instruction should be. Practical, flexible, resilient, useful, but still designed to unleash the creative spirit, to give the imagination a platform for creating wondrous work.

I held the first Red Sneaker Writers conference in 2005. I invited the best speakers I knew, not only people who had published many books but people who could teach. Then I launched my small-group seminars—five intensive days with a handful of aspiring writers. This gave me the opportunity to read, edit, and work one-on-one with people so I could target their needs and make sure they got what would help them most. This approach worked extremely well and I'm proud to say a substantial number of writers have graduated from my seminars and placed work with major publishers. But I realized not everyone could attend my seminars. How could I help those people?

This book, and the other books in this series, are designed to provide assistance to writers regardless of their location. The books are short, inexpensive, and targeted to specific areas where a writer might want help.

Let me see if I can anticipate your questions:

Why are these books so short? Because I've expunged the unnecessary and the unhelpful. I've pared it down to the essential information, practical and useful ideas that can improve the quality of your writing. Too many instructional books are padded with excerpts and repetition to fill word counts required by book contracts. That's not the Red Sneaker way.

Why are you writing several different books instead of one big book? I encourage writers to commit to writing every day and to maintain a consistent writing schedule. You can read the Red Sneaker books without losing much writing time. In fact, each can be read in a single afternoon. Take one day off from your writing. Read and make notes in the margins. See if that doesn't trigger ideas for improving your work.

I bet it will. And the next day, you can get back to your work.

You reference other books as examples, but you rarely quote excerpts from books (other than yours). Why?

Two reasons. First, I'm trying to keep these books brief. I will cite a book as an example, and if you want to look up a particular passage, it's easy enough to do. You don't need me to cut and paste it for you. Second, if I quote from materials currently under copyright protection, I have to pay a fee, which means I'd need to raise the price of the books. I don't want to do that. I think you can grasp my points without reading copyrighted excerpts. Too often, in my opinion, excessive excerpting in writing books is done to pad the page count.

Why does each chapter end with exercises?

The exercises are a completely integrated and essential part of this book, designed to simulate what happens in my small-group seminars. Samuel Johnson was correct when he wrote: *Scribendo disces scribere.* Meaning: You learn to write by writing. I can gab on and on, but these principles won't be concretized in your brain until you put them into practice.

So get the full benefit from this book. Take the time to complete the exercises. If you were in my seminar, this would be your homework. I won't be hovering over your shoulder when you read this book—but you should do the exercises anyway.

What else does the Red Sneaker Writers Center do?

I send out a free e-newsletter filled with writing advice, market analysis, and other items of interest. If you would like to be added to the mailing list, then please visit: http://www.williambernhardt.com/writing_instruction/index.php. We hold an annual writing conference with a specific focus: providing the information you need to succeed. I lead small-group seminars every summer. The newsletter will provide dates and information about these programs. And there will be future books in this series.

You may also be interested in my DVD set, *The Fundamentals of Fiction*, available at Amazon or on my website. It's about five hours of me talking about writing. Who doesn't want that?

Okay, enough of this warm-up act. Read this book. Then write your story. Follow your dreams. Never give up.

William Bernhardt

CHAPTER 1: DEFINING STYLE

What is written without effort is generally read without pleasure.

Samuel Johnson

First let me establish what I mean by style. I'm not talking about writing with flair, pizazz, or a unique perspective. Those topics are more commonly what writers describe as "voice." When we discuss style, we're talking about an approach to writing that improves the effectiveness of your work. In high school you may have encountered *The Elements of Style*, a collection of generally sound (if occasionally eccentric) rules for writing. In this book, we're going to take that idea even further, establishing stylistic guidelines that work well in fiction.

Any attempt to define rules or even guidelines for writing is readily susceptible to attack. This is an art as well as a craft, after all, and how can art have rules? For any principle I pronounce, some smart English major can cite an example of a great writer who broke the rule and nonetheless produced memorable work. Still, some approaches are better, and more likely to succeed, than others. This book will suggest the stylistic techniques that are more likely to produce memorable fiction.

WILLIAM BERNHARDT

Every writer should be aware that fictional style has evolved over time. I love Victorian novels, but the writers of that era could get away with more flowery language, more exacerbated descriptions, and more intrusive omniscient meddling than writers today. The novel has only existed, as an independent literary form, for about four hundred years. We owe much to Defoe, Fielding, and Richardson, but I wouldn't recommend that a contemporary novelist attempt to imitate their style. Over time, fictional style has been refined to something that most readers would agree is more immersive and immediate and easier to follow. In the post-Hemingway universe, a more direct form of storytelling is favored, both by critics and readers.

Style is about the way we express ourselves when writing.

Individuality and the Writer

Perhaps some of you are railing against the idea that you can be told how to write. I am an *artiste*, you may be thinking, and my style is individual, so my only consideration is what's right for the work.

I am not entirely unsympathetic to this view. One of the biggest mistakes a writer can make is imitating. Some writers I know go so far as to stop reading while they're writing, or at least to avoid reading anyone with an intrusive or distinctive voice.

In this book, I won't suggest that you conform to some rigorous template, nor will I try to lock you in a creative cage. But there is a dominant style in use today, and while I can't force you to adopt it I can say that your chances of success are seriously diminished if you do not.

2

And that's not because great iconoclasts are always shunned. It's because readers like some stylistic approaches better than others. Specifically, readers tend to favor clean, readily accessible language that draws them into the story. My goal is to give you an effective, efficient framework in which you can unleash your individual voice.

Don't let your writing get in the way of the story.

Style is about writing to engage the reader's imagination. Style is about writing to immerse the reader in the story to such an extent that the reader forgets that authors (and their styles) exist. When readers tell their friends about a book they enjoyed, they go on and on about the characters and the tale told. Rarely does the average reader mention style. That doesn't mean style is unimportant. But it may mean that the best style is invisible rather than showy. And it almost certainly means that the most successful fictional style does not draw attention to itself, but rather, draws attention to the characters and the story.

David Foster Wallace was one of the most acclaimed writers of the last fifty years. Wallace was perhaps best known for his intellectual nonfiction, but he also received critical praise for his fiction, particularly his novel *Infinite Jest*. Many highbrow critics trumpeted the brilliance of that book. The only problem is—almost no one can finish it. Readers are struck by Wallace's complex sentence structure, his superior vocabulary, his wonderful way with words. But most readers bog down and give up on about page fifteen. Because lovely though the language is, it is not immersive. It does not draw readers into the story. *Infinite Jest* does have its merits, but it is not an example of how to write a story people want to read.

Perhaps this doesn't bother you. Perhaps you would be content to have a small circle of devoted readers who think you're terribly smart even though they can't finish your books. (Wallace wasn't. Tragically, he killed himself after a long battle with depression.) If so, this book may not be for you. But if you're interested in learning how to write with the effectiveness and professionalism that causes people to want to publish and read your work—you may find this useful.

In the Introduction, I mentioned that I talk to many aspiring writers at conferences. Typically, those with finished manuscripts will pitch the literary agents in attendance. And sadly, this often leads to one of two dispiriting results. In some cases, the agent is not interested at all. This suggests that the premise is not engaging. The book's central idea is not making the agent see dollar signs. In many cases, however, the intrigued agent requests the manuscript—then later rejects it. In that case, the problem is style. The agent liked the idea well enough but found fault in your execution. Vague phrases like "Just didn't grab me" are agentspeak for "You're not writing at a professional level yet." In today's publishing world, editors don't have time to do much editing. Your manuscript must be largely ready to print when you submit it.

What does it mean to be publishable? It means exemplifying—and making the most of—contemporary fictional writing style.

Writing for Readers

While it is not possible to define the one and only good approach to writing, it is possible to define what style should accomplish. If style is the way we tell our story with words, then to make the story successful, style must contain two key components.

Style should lead to extreme readability and effective writing.

First, your work must have extreme readability. You must marshal your words, sentences, and paragraphs to communicate your story clearly and immediately. Adequate readability is not good enough, not in this marketplace. There's too much competition, too much mediocre work already out there. If you want to interest a publisher, your work must be exceptional. Each sentence must go down as smoothly as a drink of water. Each paragraph must draw readers deeper into the story. Each page must hold their attention with such power that they cannot put the book down.

Second, a writing style must be effective. I'm not talking about being fancy or flowery or showy. True elegance is none of those. True elegance is the use of appropriate and interesting words, phrases, metaphors, sentences, scenes, and sequences to produce graceful, unobtrusive prose that carries the reader from one page to the next. Good style communicates the story effectively without letting interest wane or, worse yet, boring the reader.

Your goal as a fiction writer is to create an immersive world of words, one that readers look forward to entering and never want to leave. To be sure, you will accomplish some of that by creating spellbinding characters. You will accomplish some of it by implementing sound story structure and inventive plotting. But none of that will succeed if your writing style fails. If readers get bogged down, or confused, or lose interest, it won't matter what brilliant bits of character or plot lie ahead. Your readers will never get there.

Every word matters.

You must pay careful attention to each word, each sentence, each paragraph. You must write every sentence so the reader plows right through it without hitting any speed bumps. You want the reader to briskly move from one sentence to the next without giving it any conscious thought, simply absorbing and enjoying the story. When the reader hits an awkward turn of phrase, too many prepositional phrases, or an excessively complex sentence—that's a speed bump. Bad style not only fails to draw in the reader but actually distances the reader from the story.

This book will explain the style that has put many novelists on the bestseller list, both with genre fiction and literary fiction. Although style is always relative to the story being told, there is a difference between good writing and bad writing. And by the end of this book, you should know the difference.

SIZZLING STYLE

Highlights

1) Style is about the way we express ourselves when writing.

2) Don't let your writing get in the way of the story.

3) Style should lead to extreme readability and effective writing.

4) Every word matters.

Red Sneaker Exercises

1) In addition to bad writing style, poor formatting can also make a manuscript look unprofessional. Here are some standards for formatting that might help next time you're pitching an agent or editor. I'm not suggesting formatting will fix your manuscript's flaws or that there's only one way to do it, but this approach is standard and using it will show that you've done your research and know how to present yourself professionally:

a) Times New Roman, 12-point font
b) One-inch margins on all four sides
c) Double-spaced throughout
d) Left-justified
e) Indent paragraphs, and no extra space between paragraphs
f) Header in the upper right corner in this format: Last Name-Title or Important Word from the Title-Page Number.

2) Have you heard the expression: You must kill your darlings? In the writing world, this usually refers to some choice phrase that is elegant or clever or poetic, something about which the writer is quite proud. The problem is that because it's so elegant or clever or poetic it draws attention to itself, and although readers might enjoy it—it takes them out of the story. It causes them to think about you and your brilliance when they should be immersed in your tale.

Do you have any darlings in your work-in-progress? And if so, do you have the courage to do what must be done?

CHAPTER 2: GRAMMAR IS NOT STYLE

No one really knows what will be commercial, but everyone knows good writing from bad writing.

William Goldman

S ometime when I tell students we're about to discuss style, they think they're in for a long dull discourse on the rules of grammar or punctuation. They're wrong, but this mistake is understandable. When people talk about style guides, they're talking about long compendiums of rules like, famously, Strunk and White's *The Elements of Style*. But we're fiction writers, not English majors (okay, some of us may be both), so we have a different approach to the subject. Certainly we don't want to flagrantly violate conventional grammar rules (unless we're doing it for a good reason). But our primary goal is communication. Our profession is storytelling. And that makes all the difference.

Rethinking Grammar

Just to get this chapter off to a lively start, and possibly to alienate everyone reading, I thought we'd start with a little pop quiz. Don't fret. The questions are all True or False, so you have a fifty-fifty shot from the outset. Note that I'm not asking whether these rules could ever be violated, say, if you're writing dialogue for a hick character with poor grammar. I'm asking whether these are valid rules of grammar that you would normally follow when writing. Try to answer all four before you look at the answers. Ready? Okay, true or false:

1) Never begin a sentence with a conjunction.
2) Never end a sentence with a preposition.
3) Never split infinitives.
4) Never use double negatives.

Okay, finished? Ready for the answers?

They're all false. Every single one of them. Perhaps you guessed that. (Savvy test-takers will suspect any True/False question that begins with "Never" is likely false.) But do you understand why? The explanation is not: I'm writing fiction, so I can do anything I want.

The explanation is: None of these are rules of grammar. And they never were.

I don't say this because I'm a hip modern freewheeling writer urging you to throw the rules out the window because we're all creative spirits and we have to do what the muse tells us to do. I say this because these aren't rules of grammar.

You don't have to take my word for it. Anytime you want to check matters of grammar or punctuation, you should consult a style guide. The style guide in use by all American professional publications, books or periodicals (though not newspapers), including the big New York publishing houses, is *The Chicago Manual of Style*, now in its 16th edition. Read the chapter called "Grammar and Style" from start to finish. See any prohibitions against split infinitives or ending sentences with prepositions? Nope.

Did they leave that out? Yup. Because they aren't rules of grammar.

These nonexistent rules are examples of what grammarians call grammar myths, meaning many people believe they're rules and may well have been taught them in school (showing just how pervasive myths can be). But they aren't rules. Why?

Because they don't make your writing better. Because they don't necessarily improve your clarity or precision. They're just arbitrary rules that may or may not produce better work. If you'd like to read a more lengthy discourse on how these grammar myths arose, I highly recommend Patricia T. O'Connor's excellent book *Origin of the Specious* (listed in Appendix C at the end of the book).

Can't start a sentence with a conjunction? Why not? Shakespeare did, and he still has a relatively good reputation as a writer. In *Hamlet*, Horatio says about the ghost: "And then it started like a guilty thing/Upon a fearful summons." (And let's not forget "Et tu, Brute"—translated: "And you, Brutus?") You will find sentences beginning with conjunctions everywhere from Dickens to popular periodicals like *The New York Times* and *US News and World Reports*. If they can do it, why can't you—assuming it's the most effective way to start a sentence in your story?

In her book, O'Connor says this non-rule probably evolved from grammar school teachers who directed young students away from conjunctions, because for young writers just learning the language, starting a sentence this way could lead to a fragment, or it could become repetitive. If you've ever listened to kids tell stories, you know that every sentence could potentially be: "And then this happened. And then that happened," etc. But there's still no rule against it. And never was.

11

Do what works best for your story. Sometimes opening with a conjunction is an effective way of drawing readers into the next sentence without hesitation or confusion. The conjunction indicates the relationship between the last sentence and the next. For instance, "and" indicates more of the same, "but" indicates an exception to what was said before, "because" signals an explanation, and so forth. No one gets lost between the sentences.

The same is true for ending a sentence with a preposition. Mind you, I'm not saying you have to do it. There are many instances in which that construction will give your writing, and particularly your dialogue, a "hick" feel:

"Where are you at?"

Of course, the true problem here is not that I ended the sentence with a preposition. It's that I added a completely unnecessary word. "Where are you?" would have done just as well.

On the other hand, there are many instances in which ending a sentence with a preposition is common and natural, so you may not be doing your readers any favors by contorting your sentence to avoid it. If you're walking along the sidewalk and suddenly trip, you are unlikely to say, "Upon what did I trip?" unless you live in a *Masterpiece Theatre* drama. Most red-blooded Americans will say, "What did I trip on?" ending a sentence with a preposition, and not bothering anyone in the slightest. You will find sentences ending with prepositions in Milton, Chaucer, Shakespeare, and the King James Bible.

There's a famous story about Churchill that may be apocryphal, but I hope not. Churchill, in addition to being a statesman of historic import, was also a superb writer who in fact won the Nobel Prize for literature. According to legend, an editor had the temerity to alter one of his sentences so it wouldn't end with a preposition. The wise Churchill changed it back, noting in the margin, "This is ghastly interference up with which I shall not put."

Perhaps the biggest grammar myth of all is the one about split infinitives, the bane of high school students for decades. This is a particularly egregious grammar myth because it compels writers to create awkward, unnatural phrasings in service of a nonexistent rule. Worse, it's based upon a complete misunderstanding of what an infinitive actually is. Contrary to common belief, an infinitive is not a two-word phrase beginning with "to." That's an infinitive phrase, similar to a prepositional phrase but more specific. The infinitive is the simplest form of a verb. So in the famous "to boldly go," (You knew I'd get around to that one, didn't you?) the infinitive is "go." How are you going to split that? Between the "g" and the "o?"

This grammar myth purports to preclude the separation of the "to" from its object (as with separating "to" from "go" with the adverb "boldly"). Why? *Star Trek* has been sending the Enterprise "to boldly go where no one has gone before," for about fifty years, and they still haven't changed the phrasing, even though someone has surely told Paramount that this violates an alleged rule. They changed "man" to "one" to make the phrase more politically correct, but they haven't moved or removed the adverb. Why?

Because it's better this way, of course. Try it yourself. Take out "boldly," or put the word before "to" or after "go." Just doesn't pack the same punch, does it? What's the point of a rule of grammar that sucks the drama out of your writing without increasing the clarity? This rule deserves to be a myth because it doesn't make your writing better.

O'Conner explains that this myth is the result of highbrows erroneously trying to apply the rules of Latin, a Romantic language, to English, a Germanic language. Nonetheless, you will find so-called split infinitives in the work of Shakespeare, Donne, Wordsworth, and many other acclaimed writers.

Consider this sentence:

He failed entirely to comprehend it.

Okay, no intrusive adverb after the "to." But the sentence is ambiguous. Are you saying that he didn't get it entirely, or that he got it somewhat but not entirely? It's unclear. Now let's see what happens when you split the so-called infinitive:

He failed to entirely comprehend it.

This construction is far less ambiguous. Now you're saying that he got it to some degree but not altogether. By violating the nonexistent rule, you produced a better sentence.

Finally, let's consider the alleged ban on double negatives. The truth is, double negatives can be useful, if you employ them properly. As in the math world, two negatives make a positive. If I say, "I can't not buy that gorgeous iPhone," I'm saying I must buy the phone (in a comical way that disguises the fact that I'm probably throwing money away for no good reason). Sometimes lawyers in court, mindful of the rules of civility more often observed in the breach than the execution, will say something like, "Plaintiff's counsel is not unintelligent."

Which, strictly speaking, means counsel is intelligent, but it's about as fainthearted a compliment as possible.

In the world of literature and rhetoric, there's a device called *litotes*. The technical definition is "An understatement in which something is expressed by the negation of its contrary." This is an English Department way of saying you employ the double negative to understate something. In other words, instead of saying, "Scrooge McDuck was incredibly rich," you say, "Scrooge was a duck of no small means." So not only are double negatives not forbidden, there's even a cool technical term describing how they can be skillfully deployed.

None of these prohibitions are rules of grammar and they never were. Which does not mean you have to start with conjunctions and end with prepositions. It means you can, if it's the best means of telling your story.

Prescriptive vs. Descriptive

In the academic world of writing instruction, two distinct approaches are frequently advocated. One is called the prescriptive approach, and the other is the descriptive approach. As you may have guessed from the name, the prescriptive approach emphasizes knowledge of the rules. Learn the rules of grammar and punctuation and apply them. Simple, right?

Simple, if your only goal is to be a technically correct writer of dull prose, but that's unlikely to lead to success in the world of fiction.

The descriptive school puts the emphasis on the message. What's the best way to communicate what I want to say? Or, applying this to fiction, "How can I best tell my story?"

A fiction writer should make language choices by asking: How can I best tell my story?

Bear in mind that English is a relatively new language, so it's not particularly surprising that it still is evolving, and probably always will be. According to Carl Sagan's famous cosmic calendar, *Homo sapiens* have employed written language for about six thousand years. But the English language only goes back about fifteen hundred years. By comparison to most of the world's major languages, it's the new kid on the block. Small wonder there's still confusion.

When Shakespeare and his contemporaries wrote, there were no style guides to consult on language niceties (or dictionaries, for that matter). There was little discussion of English grammar until the eighteenth century, and even then it was scattered, mostly people like Jonathan Swift complaining that we did not have enough words to express everything he wanted to express. This led to the importation of words from other languages, primarily Latin and Greek. What we did not import, however, were their rules of grammar.

When I suggest that your primary focus should not be grammar, I'm not suggesting that grammar is of no importance. What I'm saying is that, in my experience, anyone in love with books enough to want to write one probably already has a competent grasp of grammar and punctuation. Professional grammarians tell me that there are about twenty-five hundred rules in the English language. How many can you name? Probably not that many. But not knowing their names doesn't mean you don't understand them. Consider this sentence:

Mine daughter has blonde hair.

I'm betting most of you have already picked up on the fact that there's something wrong here. It should start with "My," not "Mine," right?

But why?

Probably few of you responded with a long discussion of the difference between the effective and relative positions of pronouns. Which is fine. All that matters is that you understand that the first construction will make your readers stop and scratch their heads, while the latter will keep them reading smoothly. And that's what you want. Leave the technical names to professors. You're a writer. Take your instinctive grasp of the language and focus on the descriptive approach to writing. In other words, tell your story as effectively as possible.

When Grammar Counts

Does that mean that grammar and punctuation are of no importance to a fiction writer? Of course not (although after reading some of the stuff that's out there from people like Joyce and Faulkner, you might wonder). There are still rules that are in fact rules, and for good reason. Because they will increase the ready communication and effectiveness of your prose.

Time for another quiz. Take a look at the next two sentences. Are they missing anything? If so, what would that be and where would you add it?

William focused on bookkeeping management and supervision. (Hint: This is a list of three items.)

The fifty page story was too long for the twelve member panel of judges.

17

In the first sentence, you probably realized that it all comes down to the commas. Does it need one or two or does it even matter?

Most of you probably put a comma after "bookkeeping," since I told you it was a list of three items. But what about the comma that comes before "and," commonly called the "Oxford comma" or the "serial comma?" Some may have heard that you put it in, that you don't, or that it's optional. What do the style guides say?

Always use the Oxford comma.

Why? Because that's how you indicate how many items are in the list, and by doing so, you increase the clarity of your sentence. Absent commas, "bookkeeping management and supervision" could all be one department. Or "management and supervision" could be one department. Employing the Oxford comma increases the immediate understanding and readability of your work. This is a rule that should be a rule, because it improves the clarity of your writing.

Granted, there are some sentences in which it will make little difference whether you use the Oxford comma or you don't. But there's no down side to using it. On this subject, *The Chicago Manual of Style* opines that there are many sentences that will be improved by using the Oxford comma, and none in which it detracts. So why not just get in the habit of using it?

You're probably familiar with the famous Robert Frost poem, "Stopping by Woods on a Snowy Evening." You probably also recall the haunting opening of the final stanza:

The woods are lovely, dark and deep,

18

But I have promises to keep…

Wait a minute. Shouldn't there be an Oxford comma in that first line? Good question. When the poem first appeared, there was no Oxford comma. When the poem was later reprinted in Frost's own anthology, the Oxford comma appeared. Does it make a difference?

Definitely. Without the comma…

The woods are lovely, dark and deep…

…there's no list. "Dark" and "deep" explain why the woods are lovely. Loveliness is defined as darkness and deepness. But with the Oxford comma, the sentence becomes a list, and the meaning changes:

The woods are lovely, dark, and deep…

Now we have a chain of three adjectives modifying "woods." The woods are lovely, and dark, and deep. The meaning of what Frost is saying, and its impact on the rest of the poem, changes dramatically. Believe me, English majors have been writing papers about that comma for about eighty years now. So it must be important.

Give your readers a break. Use the Oxford comma where appropriate.

The second sentence similarly involves a rule that should be a rule because it increases the immediate clarity of your work. You probably realized that this sentence contains two phrasal adjectives (even if you've never heard the term "phrasal adjectives"). Traditionally, when two or more words combine to make a single adjective, we

19

hyphenate them, to make clear that these words go together. So the better way to write this sentence would be:

The fifty-page story was too long for the twelve-member panel of judges.

Does it make a difference? Yes. Readers are often confused by long strings of adjectives. By including the hyphens, you help them sort out the sentence so they don't puzzle over your prose. "Fifty" doesn't modify story. It modifies "page." You communicate that to the reader by including the hyphen.

Consider the following (based upon a real-life headline):

EMT TEAM HELPS DOG BITE VICTIM

Did your eyebrows rise the first time you read that? Perhaps you even chuckled…and then you reread it and understood what the writer intended. That's exactly what you don't want your readers to do. You want them to understand exactly what you mean the first time they read the sentence—and then to keep on reading. And this problem could have been solved with a simple hyphen:

EMT TEAM HELPS DOG-BITE VICTIM

Here's another headline to contemplate:

GOVT OVERSEERS FIND UNDUE INFLUENCE FROM SMALL BUSINESS LOBBYISTS

Am I the only one who imagines itty-bitty lobbyists running around Washington? Do your readers a favor and eliminate even momentary confusion (or unintended humor) by including the hyphen:

GOVT OVERSEERS FIND UNDUE INFLUENCE FROM SMALL-BUSINESS LOBBYISTS

Hyphenate phrasal adjectives.
This is far from a complete list of punctuation rules that matter, but I hope you get my point.
Focus on immediate clarity and precision.
Worry less about half-forgotten rules and focus more on implementing the stylistic approaches that will keep your reader engaged.

The Evolution of Language

One last point before we move on. What word—and it can only be one word—would you put in the blank to complete this sentence?

A writer is often judged by the quality of _____ prose.

Hmm. This one's a bit thorny, isn't it? Most of you are probably aware that writers come in two genders, so perhaps your first thought was "his or her." But I said you could only have one word (because "his or her" is awkward and clunky). Perhaps you added "one's," which is technically correct, but way too raised-pinky for my taste.
So what's the answer?

The answer is "their."

I can hear your outrage. Wait a minute, you're saying. "Their" can only be used as a plural pronoun.

Okay, then what singular possessive pronoun do we have that is gender-neutral?

And the answer is, the English language doesn't have one. And maybe that was okay back in the days of Shakespeare, but today, when women are equal partners in the workplace and other arenas, it is unforgivable. So do we go on rearranging sentences awkwardly to avoid the problem, or do we do something about it?

Most grammarians (though admittedly not all) think it is time to do something about it. And their solution is to permit the use of "their" in both singular and plural contexts. Just as another pronoun, "you," can be either singular or plural.

This isn't just my wacky idea. Google around—you'll find scores of articles on the subject. If you can't live with it, go on rewriting your sentences to avoid the problem or continue using the clumsy "his or her." But I'm raising this linguistic problem for a reason.

Language is not static. Language evolves over time.

Everything else evolves. Why wouldn't language? Other nations, notably France, have established institutes to preserve the language and protect it from the encroachment of other languages. And it never works. We are a global community and cross-pollination is inevitable. And never is change more certain than in cases like this, where there's a gap in the language that needs to be filled.

So what's my point?

It's good to know rules, especially rules that will improve the ready comprehension of your work. But if you see the need for change, for improvement, for innovation—do it.

All literary changes start somewhere. I'm not talking about change for change's sake. We've all seen enough literary novels that omit quotation marks or capital letters or use endless run-on sentences, showy style choices that all too often accomplish nothing but attracting attention to themselves. But if you devise something innovative that makes your story better, don't hesitate. Do it. And let the critics be damned. You're an artist. There's much more to being an artist than following rules.

Anytime you're unsure about a stylistic choice, ask yourself this question: What will cause my story to have the greatest impact on the reader?

Highlights

1) A fiction writer should make language choices by first asking: How can I best tell my story?

2) Always use the Oxford comma.

3) Hyphenate phrasal adjectives.

4) Focus on immediate clarity and precision.

5) Language is not static. Language evolves over time.

6) Anytime you're unsure about any stylistic choice, ask yourself this question: What will cause my story to have the greatest impact on the reader?

Red Sneaker Exercises

1) Did you get a queasy feeling when you read my assertion that most people attempting to write a book already have an instinctive grasp of grammar? You're not alone. For many, it's been a long time since grammar school and any rigorous grammar instruction. I personally never get "lay" and "lie" right. I've learned to look it up. Microsoft Word's Grammar Checker is better than it used to be, but not something upon which a writer should depend. You could consider auditing a class at a local community college, or taking an online course. You can subscribe to Grammar Girl's free emails (Google it) and read some of the books listed in the Bibliography at the end

of this book. Don't let insecurity about grammar keep you from writing the story you were meant to write.

2) If you're serious about being a writer, you need to get the most recent edition of *The Chicago Manual of Style*, either in paper or digital form. Read the chapter on "Grammar and Style." Learn anything? I certainly did the first time I read it. For that matter, I learn something new and useful every time I reread it.

CHAPTER 3: THE ESSENCE OF ART

Simplicity, simplicity, simplicity! ... We are happy in proportion to the things we can do without.

Henry David Thoreau

A t the height of his fame, Albert Einstein was asked to explain the secret of his genius. He provided three "rules of work," and the first was: "Out of clutter find simplicity." We writers may not be scientists, but this is a terrific description of what the best of us do. The essence of the art of writing is simplicity. And by simplicity I do not mean dumbing it down or writing for the lowest common denominator. I mean streamlining your prose to make it essential and powerful, with no wasted words but every word doing exactly what it should to achieve the maximum possible impact.

Embracing Your Inner Simplicity

Leonardo da Vinci seems about as far from being a simpleton as it is possible to be, and yet he wrote: "Simplicity is the greatest sign of sophistication." He would've made a fine fiction writer (an easy bet, since he was brilliant at everything else). His words have much to do with the art of writing. Too often overeager writers, anxious to display their gifts, their vocabulary, or their literary sensibilities, pour on the words and stretch out the sentences. What they don't realize is that anyone can do that. Logorrhea is easy. Spare and precise writing is much more challenging.

The direct, simplest approach is almost always the best. If you're thinking that writing complex (if not convoluted) sentences is more literary, or proves that you are a deeper and more profound artist, you are probably heading for a world of hurt the first time you try to publish. And this is not because editors are all hacks or publishers are commercial sellouts. It's because good writing is harder than bad writing—and less showy. Too often, excessive wordiness is a sign of insecurity, the equivalent of the Napoleonic complex for writers.

Consider what works well for advertising slogans, a form of writing that, if not exactly literary, nonetheless requires talent and often has enormous sums of money riding on it. Can you recall the famous advertising slogan for Nike?

Chances are, you can.

Just do it.

Hard to get much simpler than that. And yet, those three little words helped that company make billions. Why?

The truth is, this phrase is broad enough to have different meanings for different readers, but there is a general attitude of rebellion, or living fearlessly, or living life to the fullest. In the world of fiction, we might call this the theme, but here we'll be content to call it a great way to get people to shell out for expensive sneakers. The slogan suggests that wearing these sneakers proves, not just that you have disposable income, but that you are a great iconoclast, a free spirit, sticking it to the man.

When your words suggest a theme that appeals to your reader, you tend to get a positive response.

Okay, let's try another one. As I write this, Subway is the fastest growing fast-food chain in America. What's their oft-repeated slogan?

Eat fresh.

This is even simpler than the Nike slogan, but it seems to work. Subway knows they can't underprice their competitors. And sadly, most will find the ubiquitous burger and fries a little tastier. So what card is left to play?

Health. Ironic, given that this is a fast-food restaurant, but it's an approach that's made them billions.

Would it be possible to express this slogan in greater detail? Sure. They could say: "Eat at Subway's because if you keep going to McDonald's and eating that fried food you'll die young." But instead, they pare it down to two words that say essentially the same thing, only better.

Perhaps you're thinking, sure that's advertising, time is money, they have to keep it brief, but that's not applicable to what I do because in fiction I can use as many words as I want. Fine, don't trust me, trust Shakespeare. Here's a question: In all of the Bard's work, all thirty-seven (arguably) plays and more than a hundred and fifty sonnets, what's the most famous line?

To be or not to be...

Pretty simple, huh? Six words of two and three letters. Not complex as such, but brilliantly chosen words that say exactly what he wanted them to say, nothing more nor less. Simplicity, yes, but simple-minded, no. To the contrary, these six little words ask the ultimate question, the one Hamlet struggles with for the better part of five acts—one many people ask themselves at one point or another. Should I go on living this difficult, often painful life, or should I give it up and be at rest? Shakespeare is expressing extremely complex thoughts, but in the simplest possible language. Which is what makes the phrase so memorable. Shakespeare has contributed more entries to Bartlett's Famous Quotations than any other single author, and yet the phrase we remember best is composed of six simple words.

Brevity is more powerful than wordiness.

Burying your reader under a mountain of words is not the best way to write. Suggesting an idea, or a theme, is almost always better than hammering readers over the head with it. If you can write dialogue that suggests what the characters are not saying, people can read between the lines. When your description leaves room for readers to exercise their own imaginations, they will probably enjoy the book more.

Thomas Jefferson once wrote: "The most valuable of talents is that of never using two words when one will do." I concur, especially for novelists. The talented writer will learn to do more with less. That means simpler, more direct sentences. Shorter paragraphs, comprising shorter chapters. Never letting the pace drag. Never letting the reader's attention wander, not even for an instant.

Perhaps you think this sounds easier than writing in the old-fashioned, wordy, detailed, Henry-James way, taking a page and a half to describe someone's nose, etc. You are dead wrong. It's much harder. Editing yourself down to the essential is far more difficult. Mark Twain once started a missive to a friend, "I didn't have time to write a short letter so I'm writing a long one instead." Writing with brevity and concision, without sacrificing content or emotion, requires conscious effort, organizational skill, and much, much editing. In other words, it's hard work. But it's worth it. Because perhaps more than any other single factor, in the twenty-first century, this is what separates those who get published from those who do not.

Unburdening Your Sentences

Take a look at the following two sentences:

Short sentences are more effective.

Short sentences are more effective because they have dramatic impact, greater clarity, improved readability, and are far more likely to capture the reader's attention.

Given the previous discussion urging brevity, you've probably already guessed that I prefer the first construction. It's simpler, more direct, right to the point. Why use twenty-four words when you can get by with only five? But you may be thinking, yes, the first sentence is shorter, but the second one provides more detail. The second sentence explains why short sentences are more effective, and I want to express that important information.

Fine. But may I suggest a different approach?

Short sentences have more dramatic impact. They are easier to understand. They read faster. They will capture your reader's attention.

To me, this construction, where the ideas are broken down into short simple sentences, rather than conflated in a long list, is more powerful. Each period hammers home your message. The reader collects each thought, grasps it, and moves on. Sure, you don't want every sentence in your novel to begin with the same words or to be exactly the same length. Over the course of your novel there will be more variety. It's okay here (for three sentences) when it's clear you're doing it deliberately for rhetorical effect. In fact, the repetition gives your sentences a hypnotic, almost poetic feel that intensifies the passage.

Short sentences can be enormously powerful.

You have probably noticed that writers of popular fiction favor short sentences, and never more so than when they want to quicken the pace. If something exciting is happening, the sentences are likely to shrink. You may even see sentences in which a single brief, powerful sentence is the entire paragraph. Why? The combination of brevity and separation casts a spotlight on the sentence, increasing the impact it has on the reader. Next time you're reading something by Stephen King or Steve Berry, watch how the sentences shrink when something exciting happens.

> He heard something.
> He peered into the darkness.
> Red eyes peered back at him.
> He ran.

See how quickly that read? Remember that there is often more to reading than the words on a page. There is also a visual aspect. Eye appeal matters. Your average reader picks up a book at the store, opens it to a random page, glances at it for a few seconds, then decides whether to buy it. If that reader opens it and sees long blocky paragraphs, little dialogue, narrow margins, and not much white space, the book looks rather formidable and is likely to be put back on the shelf. On the other hand, if the reader sees dialogue, short paragraphs, lots of white space, the book is far more likely to be bought. That reader may never consciously think in any great detail about why they made their decision, but the visual appeal of the page was a factor.

As I write this, the bestselling author in America, by far, is James Patterson. In fact, his annual income is almost twice that of the next author in line. This is in part due to the skillful use of collaborators who allow him to produce several books in different genres per month. But it is also attributable to the distinctive Patterson style. Even when ghosts or co-authors write his books, the Patterson style is always in play. And what is the primary hallmark of this astoundingly successful style?

Brevity. Short sentences, short paragraphs, short chapters. The book flies by, never once releasing the reader from its spell. Patterson's success could be the secret to your success, too.

Don't Do the Overdo

Aspiring writers are never so tempted to overwrite as when they describe something in the narrative voice. This is when the worst instincts toward purple prose often emerge.

Here's a sample that, while not actually taken from a manuscript, is not at all unlike what I've seen in the past:

> The pullet, heavy with ennui from its mind-numbing day of harvesting maize and butterweed, bobbing its razor-sharp beak to and fro with its spasmodic gait, intermittently hopped its way over the baked soil and deeply rutted dirt causeway in the process of securing comfort and tranquility in the secure confines of the master's barbed-wire coop.

Or...

> The chicken crossed the road.

I hope you got a chuckle out of the first version. Maybe I'm exaggerating a bit, but that's the sort of thing I often see in my small-group seminars when writers, particularly those aspiring to be literary, start piling on the words. Unfortunately, there are few readers who have patience for that sort of thing these days. Novels are ultimately a narrative form, and although some may not require a rapid-fire pace, you must maintain reader interest. Verbose writing is all too likely to lose the reader's attention, even if it is beautifully written.

Perhaps you love the great Victorian-era novelists who tended to write more effusively than is common today. I do too, but I wouldn't want to try to sell one of those novels in today's market, not even to a small literary press. We must accept the fact that, just as language has evolved, so has the novel. Over time, novelists have learned how to make their stories more engaging, out of necessity, because novels have so much more competition these days. In the

Victorian era, novel-reading was the primary leisure-time activity of the leisure class. Today, novels face stiff competition from television, movies, video games, pop music, and perhaps the greatest time-waster in the history of humanity, the Internet. If novelists cannot hold a reader's attention, they cannot realistically expect to have a large readership. So epistolary novels and omniscient viewpoint have largely faded from the scene in favor of more engaging forms and faster-paced modes of storytelling. I don't consider this a sign that today's readers have shorter attention spans. I think the novel itself has evolved and writers over the centuries have learned what works best.

You've probably heard the great Elmore Leonard's first and foremost rule for writing: "Try to leave out the parts readers tend to skip." Long-winded descriptive passages are frequently skipped. And the second version of the chicken sentence, though admittedly less descriptive, does a better job of moving the story forward without letting the pace be dulled by excessive verbiage that contributes little or nothing to the story.

Don't over-describe anything.

Even though opinions may vary as to what constitutes overwriting, this remains a good rule of thumb for writers. Don't over-describe setting, or action, or characters, or anything else. When I wrote the first Ben Kincaid novel (*Primary Justice*), the first time I had Ben enter a courtroom, in my innocent naiveté, I spent a full page describing the place. My editor cut every single word, scribbling in the margin, "Everyone knows what a courtroom looks like."

It's true. In the nineteenth century, lengthier descriptions might have been justifiable, because everyone didn't know what everything looked like. But today, due to

35

the magic of television (I'm being sarcastic), there's not much most people haven't seen, at least up on a screen. So skip unnecessary words and advance the story.

Another major benefit of writing in a sparer manner is that you leave readers room to use their own imaginations. That's good. The more readers put into a book, the more they are likely to take away. So don't describe every little nuance, hand gesture, physical movement, or vocal inflection. Use direct, verb-driven, active sentences that get straight to the point. Let readers fill in the blanks.

The first words to eliminate are the modifiers, the adjectives and adverbs. The fewer of those you can get by with, the better. Truth is, most will have little impact on readers who have already envisioned a character or situation in their mind's eye and don't particularly want your modifiers messing it up for them. Here's another great Mark Twain quote (and this time, he was writing to a twelve-year old boy): "When you catch an adjective, kill it. No, I don't mean utterly, but kill most of them—then the rest will be invaluable."

Twain is so right. One well-placed killer dead-on-target adjective can have enormous impact. Forty of them won't. Too often stacking adjectives and adverbs is the lazy writer's substitute for choosing the right word, piling on the first words that come to mind rather than striving to find the perfect one.

Use modifiers sparingly.

Perhaps the most egregiously overused modifiers are the so-called degree adverbs: very, pretty, quite, rather, somewhat, truly, really, clearly, kind of, sort of, etc. They're called degree adverbs because they supposedly increase or decrease the intensity of the verb they modify, but in fact

36

they have little impact on readers. They're just words, and almost always superfluous.

Avoid degree adverbs.

Anytime you find yourself tempted to use one of these degree adverbs, take a moment to come up with a more precise verb. Instead of writing that your character was "quite happy," write that she was "thrilled" or "ecstatic." You've used fewer words and written a better, more powerful sentence. Instead of writing that your hero was "very tired," write that he was "exhausted" or "spent." Don't write that the price was "pretty reasonable." Write that it was "inexpensive." Get the idea?

The most abused degree adverb is "very." Does "very happy" impart a greater sense of happiness than "happy?" Seems to me happy is happy, and "very" is just a space waster. In his classic book on nonfiction (*On Writing Well*), William Zinssler argued that "Every little qualifier whittles away some fraction of trust on the part of the reader." He's right. Too often, writers use these modifiers to hedge their bets ("somewhat" or "rather") or to disguise their inability to come up with a stronger word ("really" and "truly"). That's not the Red Sneaker way. You've worked hard at your art and your craft. You can do better. So eliminate these useless words from your writing vocabulary. Show that you have the courage of your authorial convictions and don't need to equivocate. Don't be "rather" bold.

Be bold.

WILLIAM BERNHARDT

Highlights

1) Brevity is more powerful than wordiness.

2) Short sentences can be enormously powerful.

3) Don't over-describe anything.

4) Use modifiers sparingly.

5) Avoid degree adverbs.

Red Sneaker Exercises

1) Scan the first chapter in your work-in-progress. Do any examples of wordiness jump out at you? Do you see words that could be eliminated with little or no loss to the narrative? Don't fool yourself into thinking every word you write is sacrosanct. Everyone can be edited beneficially.

2) Use the Find and Replace function to search for the word "very." How many hits did you get? Is the number shocking? Fortunately, thanks to modern technology you can take them all out with a single click and your book will be better for it. Then you can search for the other degree adverbs. In some cases, you may find it beneficial to replace both the adverb and the verb, substituting a stronger verb that needs no adverb to get its message across.

3) Microsoft Word also has a function that allows you to check the reading level of your work. If it says your novel is composed at a college-reading level, that's not a

compliment, nor does it indicate how smart you are. More likely than not, you're using long words and long complex sentences, and that will impair the readability and thus the salability of your book. See if you can't simplify what you've written, without eliminating the complexity of your ideas. Express them in a more direct manner, applying the principles laid out in this and subsequent chapters.

CHAPTER 4: CLARITY AND PRECISION

One should use common words to say uncommon things.

Arthur Schopenhauer

The gulf between what a writer means to say and what comes out in the first draft is wider than the Royal Gorge. Why is that? Why does what seems precise in our brains often come out so fuzzy? Scientists say that Homo sapiens are language-based creatures. Indeed, our use of language may be what defines us and makes us unique. We can't grasp an idea until we can put it into words. Muddled writing is often the product of muddled thought.

"Writing is thinking," I once heard David McCullough say. "To write well is to think clearly. That's why it's so hard." The upside of this, though, is that putting ideas down on paper gives us an opportunity to refine them, to tease out meanings, and to make them better. That's one of the chief pleasures of the writing process.

English, the new kid on the language block, is fraught with opportunities for misunderstanding. We have homonyms, homophones, homographs, and about a thousand other ways to inadvertently create confusion. If we want our readers to have a smooth reading experience, to coast down the page without effort, we must work hard to eliminate these potential speed bumps. The art of writing is the art of expressing clearly and precisely exactly what we mean to say.

In writing, clarity is everything.

Taking More Time

Don't beat yourself up if your prose isn't perfectly concise and trimmed to the nub the first time you write it. Neither is mine, and I've been writing for a long time. After you've turned writing into a daily habit, some of this will come more instinctively. But there will always be a need for editing and revision. I mention this here as a word of comfort. Writing is not brain surgery—you don't have to get everything right on the first attempt.

Unfortunately, more and more I find people unwilling to revise, or purportedly lacking the time to revise, or feeling it's unnecessary. For years I was president of a regional press, and we frequently received submissions that were obviously someone's first draft. Sometimes they even admitted it in their cover letters, adding something like, "…but if you're interested, I'd be willing to do some revision." Gee, thanks.

Word processors are a great gift to the serious writer, but they have also made it too easy for the amateur to write quickly with insufficient thought and planning. People type out email messages and hit Send without even rereading them, and the next thing you know they're writing everything that way. Sadly, even the major publishing houses are now encouraging their top talents to "write fast." The eBook revolution appears to have created a surge in impulse buying, so publishers that once limited their authors to one book a year are now encouraging them to kick out two or even three books a year. I don't have to tell you what happens to the quality of someone's work when they're spitting out novels at that pace. Even if they work with ghostwriters or co-writers, it means less time to contemplate, plan, and revise—and the result will be a subpar book.

Perhaps after reading the discussion in the previous chapter you thought, gee, if my goal is to write more simply, with fewer words and shorter paragraphs, then writing this novel will take less time and require less revision, right?

Totally wrong. In fact, it's just the opposite. Remember what Mark Twain said.

It takes more time to write less.

That might seem counterintuitive, but it's true. You must go over each sentence, weighing the need and effectiveness of every word. That takes time. But ultimately, that's the difference between a great novel and an adequate novel.

Streamlining your work can be tricky because those words on the page may exist for different reasons. Typically, redundant information that tells readers something they already know should be cut, but it's always possible you're providing subtext, giving the reader background information, or creating a voice. In most cases, I would urge readers to accomplish those goals without running in place, that is, bringing the story to a standstill. But I realize that isn't always possible. So every word becomes a debate.

Choose each word carefully.

John Updike once said that when he wrote, he chose each word as if he might be hauled into court to defend the selection. This is an excellent description of the painstaking process of writing and revision. No word is chosen by accident, or simply because it's the first word that popped into the writer's head. Every word is chosen for a purpose by a writer with an eye on the big picture, the book as a whole. Kurt Vonnegut said that when he edited, he went through the manuscript word by word, considering whether each word had to be there. Not whether it *could* be there. Whether it *had* to be there. If it wasn't necessary, he cut it. This is a high standard, but it resulted in spare yet amazingly effective storytelling, rich in character and heavily laden with theme.

The Pursuit of Precision

The English language, even more than most, is laden with potential problems for the unwary writer. Sometimes ambiguities can be humorous, which is great if you're a standup comic, though not so terrific if you're writing a novel. If you read my book on Dialogue, you're already aware of my devotion to Burns and Allen. George and Gracie performed some hilarious routines. Typically, the humor was at Gracie's expense and revolved around some ambiguity created by the multiple meanings of words or Gracie's tendency to take idiomatic language literally. Here are a few choice examples:

Gracie: You can't eat these peaches, it's twelve o'clock!

Harry Morton: What has that got to do with anything?

Gracie: It says right here: should serve from two to four.

Or another…

Real Estate Agent: I presume the bedrooms are upstairs.
Gracie: Yes, except when you're upstairs. Then they're on the same floor.

Or my all-time favorite:

George: Well, Gracie, any news from home?
Gracie: Yes. I got a letter from my little niece, Jean.
George: What did she say?
Gracie: She didn't say anything. She didn't phone. It was a letter, and she wrote it.
George: I mean what did she write?
Gracie: It's spring again, and my family is putting on a backyard circus, just like we did when I was a kid.
George: Every spring you kids used to put on your own circus?
Gracie: Yes. Of course, admission was free, but that was only for the people who could afford it.

Yes, funny when they do it, but much less so when it creeps unintentionally into your novel. The optimist might say, Well, you've given your reader a chuckle, but what you've actually done is yank your reader out of the story. They're thinking about the author now. That's not the way to write a spellbinding story that tugs the reader from one page to the next, or for that matter, from one book to the next. You want to write prose that is so precise it's perfectly understood the first time readers read it, without any misunderstandings, comic or otherwise. So when writing and editing, watch for potential misunderstandings or ambiguities.

Unintended ambiguities will pull your reader out of the story.

See You in the Funny Papers

Fiction writers are not the only ones who can be plagued by unintended misreadings of their prose. It happens to newspaper writers all too frequently, probably because the breakneck pace of a daily paper does not permit as much reflection and revision as might be advisable. These unintended flubs can result in readers laughing over what is in fact a grim scenario, as in the following case. This is an actual printed headline for a story about famine in Angola.

STARVING ANGOLANS EATING DOGS, BARK

Did you have to read that one twice? Did you have to stifle a laugh? I think the article intended to relate the grim news that these people were so hungry they ate tree bark. But bark is a homonym, a word with two distinct meanings. One of the great discoveries of the experienced writer is that not only the choice of words but the position of words, the juxtaposition of words, can influence the way a reader understands it. Put the word "bark" beside the word "dogs" and most people will think of the wrong kind of "bark."

The next one's even worse. You've heard of the Make-A-Wish program sending children with serious illnesses to DisneyWorld, right? Here's the real-life headline:

DISNEY KEEPS TOUCHING KIDS

Can you imagine the face of the Disney CEO who's expecting a nice puff piece he can cut and paste into the annual report...but instead sees this headline. Ouch. Not going to the shareholders.

And no one at the newspaper foresaw this problem? Obviously, "touching" has multiple meanings. Sadly, in this day and age, if you juxtapose the word "touching" with the word "kids," most people's minds will go in an ugly direction.

Remember the little boy who floated from Cuba to Florida, igniting a huge debate over whether he should be sent back? Here's the headline:

CUBANS MARCH OVER 6-YEAR OLD

Okay, this time you're allowed to laugh. "Marching" can mean protest-marching, and "marching" can mean they trampled the poor kid. You know it was the former, but the other possibility still crosses your mind.

Here's my all-time favorite:

WILLIAM KELLY, 87, WAS FED SECRETARY

You know, people of advanced years just get hungrier...

WILLIAM BERNHARDT

Perhaps you recall your English teacher warning you about the dangers of dangling participles. Perhaps at the time you thought this was of no great importance. Perhaps this writer did too...

In Oklahoma City, the "in" place for years has been Ziff's for corned beef. Thinly sliced and heaped on rye, corned beef lovers won't be disappointed.

What if they don't want to be thinly sliced?

The dangling clause should modify the first sentence, not the last part of the last sentence. Of course, if the writer had been composing with more directness and simplicity, he might've dropped the unneeded clause altogether.

For years, people have collected similar examples of unexpected laughter arising from imprecision, poor writing, poor proofreading, or inattention to detail—in church bulletins. Here are a few of my favorites:

Ladies, don't forget the rummage sale. It's a chance to get rid of those things not worth keeping around the house. Bring your husbands.

Don't let worry kill you off—let the church help.

Harold Barton and Jess Caldwell were married on October 24 in the church. So ends a friendship that began in their school days.

The eighth graders will be presenting Shakespeare's *Hamlet* in the church basement Friday night. The congregation is invited to attend this tragedy.

SIZZLING STYLE

The Associate Minister unveiled the church's new tithing campaign last Sunday: "I Upped My Pledge—Up Yours."

The Source of Ambiguity

As all these examples make clear, ambiguity can arise from many different sources. Here's a checklist, so you can be on your guard for them:

Homonyms, Homographs, Homophones

Apparently, as English evolved, rather then coming up with new words for new ideas, people tended to recycle the old ones. That has created no end of problems, as you saw in some of the preceding headlines.

Homonyms are usually defined as words that share the same spelling and pronunciation, but have different meanings (like "bark" in the Angolan headline).

Homographs are words that share the same spelling but have different pronunciations, such as "permit" when used as a noun and "permit" when used as a verb. Listen to the difference in this sentence: Permit me to get you a permit. The accent is on different syllables. The "bow" you use to launch an arrow and the "bow" you take after a performance have different middle phonemes.

Homophones are words that share the same pronunciation but may be spelled differently, such as "there," "their," and "they're," or "to," "too," and "two."

And if you're really interested, English also has heteronyms (same spelling, different pronunciation and meaning), heterographs (same pronunciation, different meaning and spelling), polysemes (same spelling, possibly different pronunciation, different but related meaning), and capitonyms (words that have different meanings and possibly different pronunciations when capitalized, like "polish" and "Polish"), though these are less frequently causes of ambiguity.

I find myself repeatedly switching homonyms in my first drafts, even embarrassingly daft substitutions like "no" instead of "know." No worries (or perhaps, Know worries). That's what second drafts are for. Just make sure they aren't in your final draft.

Confusing Parts of Speech

When a word is more commonly used in one particular way, and you choose to employ it in a different way, misunderstanding often results, even if it is only momentary. In most circumstances, the savvy writer will choose to express the thought a different way rather than risk confusing the reader. Confused readers tend not to get wrapped up in the story, but rather become frustrated and eventually put down the book.

One obvious example would be gerunds, words ending with –ing that are used as nouns. Normally, when readers see an –ing word, they expect it to be a verb, so they may be thrown, if only for a moment, when you use it otherwise.

Skating around the park is one of my favorite activities.

Eating in front of the television can be a fun way to spend the evening.

In both cases, the use of the gerund as subject may cause the reader to retrace their steps, to read the sentence a second time to fully understand it. Which is exactly why I wouldn't write it that way.

Inappropriately juxtaposed words

Both the Angolan headline and the Disney headline demonstrate the danger of placing words with multiple meanings beside other words that may subconsciously influence the reader's interpretation. Be careful where you place words with multiple meanings (or avoid using them.)

The placement of words is just as important as the choice of words.

Denotations and Connotations

Denotation is the dictionary definition of a word, the literal meaning. Connotation is a subtext that arises, a cultural or emotional association. For example, "strong-willed" and "pig-headed" both have the same denotation. The both basically mean "stubborn." But as every parent knows, stubbornness is sometimes a desirable characteristic and sometimes not. Despite having the same denotation, "strong-willed" has a positive connotation, but "pig-headed" has a negative one.

Connotations rise and fall over time and a writer must be sensitive to them—especially writers who expect their work to be read for a long period of time. A good example is the word "notorious." Originally, this word simply meant "famous." It has the same root as "noteworthy." But over time, a different meaning arose, primarily because Hoover and others at the FBI in the early twentieth century used the word to describe felons like Dillinger and Pretty Boy Floyd. Consequently, "notorious" acquired a negative connotation, meaning "famous, but for a bad reason."

Of course, the only way to be aware of popular connotations is to talk to people and to read. But it's necessary, because you want to avoid being like the

51

headline writer who apparently didn't understand what thoughts might arise when he placed the word "touching" beside the word "kids."

Abstractions

This problem arises most commonly with nouns. When you use a concrete noun referring to a tangible reference point, there is little room for confusion. You say "chair" or "desk" or "table" and every reader knows more or less what you're describing. Sure, there may be different kinds of chairs, but everyone gets the general idea. It's a piece of furniture a character can sit upon. So the use of the word is unlikely to slow or confuse the reader and will conjure the mental image you intend.

Now what happens when you use a more abstract noun, such as "truth" or "honor" or "professional?" Obviously, these words can have different meanings to different people, depending upon their backgrounds, education, and experience. Anyone who's listened to both sides of a divorce case can tell you that "truth" is more subjective than objective. "Honor" is even more idiosyncratic. People have justified murder (dueling comes to mind) in the name of defending honor, even though the dictionary definition of the word suggests something noble and uplifting. All too often "professional" is used to describe what the speaker does as opposed to what somebody else does. Writers who employ these abstractions run the risk of suggesting something to their readers other than what they intend.

I've gotten a lot of mileage out of another abstract word: "Justice." This word has appeared in the titles of about half the Ben Kincaid novels, and understandably so, since the series revolves around a lawyer and is in many ways an exploration of the American justice system. *Perfect*

Justice was meant to be ironic, as there's no such thing, at least not in this world. Indeed, I intended many of these novels to explore just how erratic and unjust our justice system could be. Nonetheless, the word is more than an abstraction to Ben, who strives, often against significant odds, to find some measure of justice for his clients. So I was able to make this abstraction work for me. But I was always careful about how I used it, well aware that what one person considers justice another may consider outrageous.

Omitted Information

One of the easiest ways to let a sentence, or even an entire novel, go astray is by leaving out a word, a sentence, or a critical bit of information. This is one of the hardest problems for writers to fix themselves and one of the best reasons for employing outside editors.

It's easy to leave something out of a first draft, even if you're working from a detailed outline. But sometimes we don't catch the omission when revising, even when the word is of critical importance to the sentence (like "not"). Why? Because your brain knows what the sentence is supposed to say, so it puts the word in even though you haven't actually typed it. This can lead to big problems.

The best security against this flaw is to get an outside reader. Or ten. Mind you, I think everyone should learn to edit themselves, and you should correct ninety-nine percent of your errors yourself. But for those elusive omissions that you don't catch, it's worth having an editor you trust who has no preconceived notion of what the sentence will say. Those readers will notice the omissions.

Semantic Change

We already discussed how language evolves over time. Nowhere is this more apparent than in colloquial language or slang. Everyday language changes at the speed of light.

Once upon a time, "bad" meant bad, but if you've had any contact with young people during the last thirty years, you may have noticed that the word can also mean "good." When Michael Jackson sang about being bad, it was a self-compliment. Words change meaning over time, and a writer must be sensitive to those changes. If you don't want your dialogue to seem dated, you should avoid slang, or better yet, invent your own (see Dynamic Dialogue).

Language can evolve over time in other ways. As I mentioned earlier, the use of "their" (or "they") as a singular pronoun is coming into use, whether you like it or not.

Let me ask you another question. If you do something that you didn't intend to do, would you say you did it "*by* accident" or "*on* accident?"

(Insert *Jeopardy!* think music.)

If you're over forty, chances are you say "by accident." But if you're under forty, you may say "on accident." There's nothing wrong with either construction. "On accident" is a perfectly good neologism. It makes perfect sense. If you did something deliberately, you'd say you did it "on purpose," right? So what's wrong with "on accident?" Nothing. It's just new. So if you're writing a character under forty, it may be the way to go.

A writer must have some fundamental connection with or understanding of any character they write, even the bad ones, and that includes understanding how they talk and what words they might use. This understanding can arise from a study of real-life people or from fleshing out completely fictional people in immaculate detail. But one way or another, they must sound real, and that requires hard work and careful attention to word choices.

SIZZLING STYLE

At first, avoiding all these potential sources of ambiguity may seem taxing, but over time it will come more naturally and readily. This is another reason to make writing a daily habit. With regular practice, you will find your brain automatically rewriting your sentences to avoid these potential problems before they make it to the page.

Highlights

1) In writing, clarity is everything.

2) Choose each word carefully.

3) Unintended ambiguities will pull your reader out of the story.

4) Homonyms, homographs, and homophones can create unintended ambiguities in your writing.

5) Confusing parts of speech can create ambiguities.

6) The placement of words is just as important as the choice of words.

7) A lack of awareness of a word's connotations can create reader misunderstandings.

8) Abstractions can cause different readers to form different interpretations of the same material.

9) Omitted information can result in a sentence that makes perfect sense to the author—but not to the reader.

10) A writer must be sensitive to semantic change.

Red Sneaker Exercises

1) After you've caught yourself switching the same homonyms more than once, start making a list. (You can

do the same with any other recurring errors.) Somewhere in the revision process, do a special Find and Replace search for your most common errors. You may save yourself some unintended embarrassment.

2) Next time you hear or read something you consider to be bad grammar, before you criticize, ask yourself, "Is it possible the language has evolved? Is this an example of semantic change?"

CHAPTER 5: HARNESSING THE LIGHTNING

Writing in English is the most ingenious torture ever devised for sins committed in previous lives.

James Joyce

I opened this book with the famous quotation from Twain about lightning and lightning bugs because it so brilliantly encapsulates everything I'm suggesting in this book. When writers can both write with simplicity and carefully choose each word for maximum impact, they start doing their most powerful work.

Don't be discouraged if this doesn't happen overnight. In some respects, writing is like everything else—the more you do the better you get. Vonnegut once said that every writer has about a million words of garbage (not precisely his word) to get out before they get to the good stuff. I'm not sure about the number, but the central idea is correct. And it's one more reason to start writing now if you're serious about being a writer, and to keep at it, day after day after day.

Lightning Bugs are Pretty, But...

Once you recognize the importance of choosing each word, you will understand just how hard writing is, and perhaps, why you didn't become an overnight success or sell the first thing you wrote. You've probably experienced the frustrating moment when you write a sentence and realize that you're not using exactly the right word—but can't think what the better word is. This might be the time to get up and take a stroll. Walk the dogs. Take a little exercise. Get some blood circulating. You may even decide to wait till later, maybe in the next draft, and see if the word comes to you then. That's fine, as long as you do in fact come back and think about it later. Otherwise, you're not doing your best possible work and you have no right to complain about not being published.

The difference between the almost right word and the right word is the difference between the lightning bug and the lightning.

And obviously, you want to harness the lightning.

The Right Word, Not More of Them

So what exactly did Mark Twain mean? Does he have a problem with lightning bugs? No. To the contrary, I think he recognized that lightning bugs are pleasant and pretty. But a writer's words must be more than pretty. A writer's words should have power and impact. They should strike like the lightning, catching the reader by surprise and making an indelible, electrifying impression.

In my novel for young readers, *The Black Sentry*, when boys reach the age of sixteen, they are forced to undergo a one-on-one public combat, the outcome of which will determine their social status for the rest of their lives. In my first many drafts, I called this "the Combat." Pretty original, huh? The scene portraying this strife was keenly dramatic, with lots of sweating and grunting and angst, but something about it never really sparked. It took outside input, the voice of a friend, to point out that as names go, "the Combat" was pretty uninspired. Several drafts later I changed it to "the Winnowing." And as simple as this change may seem, it transformed the whole scene. The stakes, the danger, even the reflection on this fictional society (with definite parallels to our own) all crystalized with a simple name change. For me, this was a classic example of employing the right word instead of the not-nearly-right word. The lightning rather than the lightning bug.

Word choice is important to any form of verbal communication. When prosecutors address the jury, they do not say, "Ladies and gentlemen, I represent the government." Sadly enough, "government" is now a super-charged word with mostly negative connotations. So you will hear, "Ladies and gentlemen, I represent the People," or "I represent the United States of America." But you'll never hear them say they represent the government—even though they do.

If you need any further examples of the import of finding the right word, consider the world of politics. This is a realm in which word choice is critical. As a general rule, politicians would much rather change a name than engage in the more difficult business of changing content. National party committees now commonly hire semantic consultants as they gear up for national elections every four years. No, not substance consultants, but semantics consultants—experts on the usage and meanings of words. The focus is on the language of the message rather than the substance. Why? Because they've learned that if you can control the vocabulary of the debate, you are far more likely to win it.

When Trent Lott first attempted to alter congressional parliamentary procedure, he referred to it as the "nuclear option," because it would obliterate the rules as they then existed. (To be fair, he was not the first or last to use the term.) Could he be surprised that senators were not eager to rally behind a "nuclear option?" When the rules were finally altered in 2013 to reduce the possibility of filibustering to block appointments, most people referred to it as the "Constitutional option" (even though there's nothing in the Constitution about congressional procedure).

Similarly, in the early days of the Affordable Health Care Act, the drafters contemplated that in some instances the government would issue health insurance to certain people. This was called "the government option." It didn't take much polling to realize that anything using the word "government" would not be popular. The name was soon changed to "the public option" and poll results improved dramatically—even though the plan itself hadn't changed at all.

When the economy first started nose-diving back in 2008, Congress scrambled for a response. The first economic aid bill, as you may recall, was commonly called the "bailout." Are you surprised that didn't pass? Who wants to back a bailout? The very word suggests someone is at fault. Losers have to be bailed out, rather than held responsible for their own actions. You bail out a sinking ship—and it's still going to sink. (Subsequently, "bailout" has become a derogatory term applied to any aid legislation proposed by the other party.)

The aid package that finally passed was called the "rescue" package. Do you see the difference? "Rescue" has a much more positive connotation. Superheroes are rescuers, and the people they rescue are victims, not losers. During the Obama administration, economic aid packages did not discontinue, but in an effort to distinguish them from previous efforts, these bills were called "stimulus packages." The word "stimulus" has a positive connotation and suggests that the goal is not to abet losers, cheats, and frauds, but to stimulate the economy, which benefits everyone. (Though to my mind, "stimulus package" still sounds like something you'd get in an adult toy store. But I guess that's just me.)

Etching Sentences with Lightning

Too often, when writers aspire to be "literary," they start pouring on the words. Long, poetic descriptions, verbose passages in which nothing much happens. This sort of writing not only fails to grab the reader but too often shows a fundamental misunderstanding of what constitutes literary fiction. The writer striving for excellence shouldn't be looking for more words, but rather, should be looking for the one perfect word that makes all the others superfluous. The writer striving for excellence should avoid the stuffy and verbose and instead use ordinary English to say something extraordinary. Too often the resort to long unfamiliar words is a sign of authorial insecurity. Remember, multi-syllabic words are the ones most frequently looked up, and few readers feel looking up words enhances their reading experience. So what's your goal? To show how smart you are, or to captivate your reader?

The same could be said of long sentences with complex or convoluted structure, sentences with long dependent clauses and prepositional phrases or worse, heaven forbid, semicolons. What the amateur writer sees as elegance the reader will see as cluttered. Your job is to clear away the clutter, all the unnecessary stuff that comes between your story and your reader. When you use fewer words and simpler structure, you increase reading speed while maximizing clarity and impact. This is the sort of writing that causes readers to stay up all night finishing a book. And those are the books they recommend to their friends, which is how bestsellers are made.

The fundamental structure of any English language sentence is subject-verb-object (if there is an object).

When you follow that pattern, with as little else as possible getting in the way, you'll write sentences that are readily absorbed and comprehended. I'm not suggesting this is the only way to write or that every sentence need follow a formula. Sure, you can put the verb first or stick a long dependent clause before the subject, but every time you do, you decrease the readability of your work a little more. The shorter, more direct way of saying something will almost always have more impact.

Just for once, to show that I am a diverse, multi-faceted person, instead of making another reference to *Star Trek*...I'll refer to *Star Wars*. You remember Yoda, right? And you probably also remember that he has an odd way of speaking. You could usually figure out what he meant, given some thought, but there still was something strange about it. What was that exactly?

What distinguished Yoda's speech was the failure to follow the aforementioned subject-verb-object pattern. Instead, he would pull the object (occasionally the verb) to the front of the sentence.

SIZZLING STYLE

Powerful, you have become.

or

Look so old do I to young eyes?

He's still speaking English, but because he's altered the standard word order, it sounds...alien. Which is exactly what the scriptwriters wanted. Yoda is not from the same planet as the rest of the characters. He's from Dagobah. Having him speak a foreign language and forcing viewers to read subtitles was too taxing a way to remind viewers of his alien status, so instead they used altered sentence structure to remind you that, sure, he may look like a Muppet, and he may sound like Miss Piggy, but he's actually an alien from Dagobah.

But here's the most interesting aspect of Yoda's dialogue. Whenever has has something of critical importance to say, something George Lucas wants to make sure you understand—he reverts to the standard subject-verb-object pattern.

The fear of loss is a path to the dark side.

or

A Jedi uses the force for knowledge and defense, never for attack.

Here's your excuse to rescreen the *Star Wars* trilogy (the good one) and see if I'm not right. The screenwriters are happy to mess with Yoda's dialogue when it doesn't much matter whether the viewer gets it or not, but when it does matter, Yoda's communication skills suddenly improve and he talks standard English. You should do the same, anytime it matters whether your readers get what you wrote. And when does it ever not?

Every Word Matters

In the course of your writing career, there will be times when you wonder whether all this revision and proofreading is necessary. After all, you've read books that had typos. The world did not come to an end. Even if you accept the importance of choosing the right word to say exactly what you intend, how much difference can a mistake here and there really make?

I have three responses. First, a novel is a contract between you and the reader. You've promised something, so you ought to deliver. Every little error whittles away at the reader's confidence (not to mention giving cranks an excuse to take a star off your Amazon review).

Second, every time a reader spots an error, it yanks them out of the story. It causes them to think about you, rather than your characters. And we've already discussed how disastrous that can be.

Third…consider the case of Neil Armstrong. You remember the first man to ever walk on the moon, don't you?

Do you remember the famous words he spoke when he first set foot on the lunar surface? Think about it before you look…

That's one small step for (a) man, one giant leap for mankind.

Chances are, when you worked from memory, you recalled it without the "a" that I inserted in parentheses. But if you Google it, you may or may not find the "a" included. Why? What did Armstrong actually say?

Considerable controversy surrounds this question. The line was written well in advance. Armstrong had practiced it. And he meant to say it with the "a." But if you listen to the actual recording…you won't hear it. Granted, the transmission came a long way and there's lots of static. It's possible something was lost. But sound engineers have worked with the recording extensively, clearing away the noise, and no one has yet detected any evidence of that stray article adjective. It would appear that Armstrong omitted a word.

Does it make any difference? After all, we know what he meant.

Or do we? Consider the sentence both ways, with and without the "a." With the "a," as intended, he's making a clear comparison. This is one step for a man, him, the guy stepping off the lunar lander, but it's a huge technological step forward for all of mankind. Meaning understood.

But if you leave out the article adjective, the statement becomes more problematic. Without the "a," it sounds as if "man" means mankind (today we would probably say "humankind" or "humanity"). At that point, the comparison no longer makes sense. It's a small step for man, it's a giant leap for man—which is it?

And thus one of the most famous statements in history, heard originally by billions and heard by billions more since, was sabotaged. By the omission of "a," the shortest non-capitalized word in the English language.

So you see, even at the macro level, word choice is of critical importance.

Keats agonized over article adjectives, too. Surviving manuscripts show that he went back and forth between the titles "To a Skylark" and "To the Skylark." Does it make any difference? It apparently did to him. If he used the definite article, "the," it sounded as if the poem pertained solely to that particular bird that happened to be posed on his windowsill one fateful morning. But Keats wanted the poem to have more universal appeal. So ultimately he decided to use the other title, "To a Skylark." This choice allowed the poem to apply to all skylarks, or perhaps, to the general idea of a skylark and what skylarks represent. "Higher still and higher/From the earth thou springest..."

I recall great controversy in the halls of fandom when the first Michael Keaton Batman picture was released. The casting of a comedian as the grim vigilante had been controversial from the start. But what particularly bothered some was the hero's introductory line. As he shakes the sniveling perp by the lapels, the man stutters, "Who are you?" Keaton replies, "I'm Batman."

Problem? In the comics of that era, the character was commonly referred to as "*the* Batman." Apparently the article adjective made him sound more dignified. After all, "Batman" wasn't his first name. It was more like a title of respect, for a character long due the proper respect. (Or perhaps they felt "*the* Batman" was necessary to distinguish him from all the other Batmen.)

"The" and "A" are the words most commonly found in titles of fiction. Does the selection make a difference? Of course. Holden Caulfield doesn't want to be just another catcher in the rye. He wants to be *The* Catcher in the Rye. Jay isn't just any old great Gatsby. He's The Great Gatsby. Don Corleone wasn't your run-o'-the-mill godfather (although in fact there were several). He's The Godfather.

68

And no self-respecting churchgoer is ever going to refer to the sacred text as "A Holy Bible." It's the one and only.

No word is unimportant. Every single one matters. So choose each one carefully.

Expunge the Unnecessary

Eliminate every word that does not convey meaning.

Every writer, at least in the first draft, will insert unnecessary words. We have a habit of falling into repetitious ways of expressing ourselves. Your choice of words will vary depending upon where you grew up or who you hang with. Lawyers have a habit of addressing the court with unnecessary words like "It should be noted that…" or "I would suggest that…" Stronger sentences would result if they dropped those words and just started the thought.

How many times have you read a business document that began "I am writing this letter for the purpose of…" or "The subject of this memo is…" Are those words necessary? The reader can see what it is and they assume it has some purpose. Cut to the chase already. Drop the unnecessary words and get to the point.

Writers sometimes fall into the bad habit of starting sentences with definite or indefinite pronouns followed by to-be verbs. This practice is not great in nonfiction and is particularly poor for fiction.

Avoid sentences beginning with "There were" or "This was" or "It was."

Of course, if you're writing dialogue and you think that's how your characters would express themselves, you at least have some justification (though it still doesn't make for good writing). But generally speaking, these

69

constructions lead to weak sentences. Pronouns should have antecedents, nouns they refer back to. If the antecedent is unclear, the sentence will be muddy.

It was a dark and stormy night.

What exactly is "it?" What does "it" refer back to? (Grammarians will say "it" is "night," which creates new problems—an antecedent that comes after the pronoun rather than before, and a subject that is identical to the object.) So you have an indefinite unclear noun coupled with a weak to-be verb (more on verbs later). Is it any wonder the sentence is dull and ineffectual? Fixing this may require revision, but in most cases, the entire problem could be solved simply by dropping the offending words and starting later in the sentence.

There were three key factors Jonathan considered before making his decision.

Or…

Three factors helped Jonathan make his decision.

Or better yet…

Jonathan considered three factors before making his decision.

The last construction makes the actor the subject of the sentence, thus eliminating the passive voice problem (discussed later), eliminating an indefinite pronoun as subject, and replacing the inert to-be verb with a stronger one. And the result is a better sentence.

Paring Away Prepositional Phrases

When trying to write with simplicity, clarity, and grace, remove prepositional phrases whenever possible. Am I suggesting that prepositional phrases are ungrammatical? No. I'm suggesting that in most sentences they represent clutter, and the more clutter you clear the stronger your sentence will be.

Remember the subject-verb-object construction that is the foundation for the English language sentence? Do you see prepositions in there anywhere? No. You can stick them in, but they will slow down your reader. And I've seen writers string five or six prepositional phrases together, not realizing how they clutter their work. Compare the following two constructions:

> Shortening your sentences of fiction by eliminating phrases of prepositions will improve your writing of narratives.

> Short sentences without prepositional phrases will improve your fiction.

Okay, you would probably never write anything so horrible as that first sentence. But compare the two. Which read more smoothly—the one laden with prepositional phrases or the one without? I hope the answer is clear. **Eliminating prepositional phrases will streamline your prose.**

71

WILLIAM BERNHARDT

Perhaps you're thinking, yes, but I have some critical information I need to get to my reader, and I can't squeeze it into a subject or a verb. Don't I need prepositional phrases? No. Happily, there are alternatives. When I edit manuscripts I would say about three-fourths of the prepositional phrases I encounter could be completely eliminated with no loss whatsoever to the story. Most of the rest could be replaced by a single word, usually a well-chosen adjective. (Notice in the sentence above how "fiction" replaces "sentences of fiction" and "prepositional phrases" replaces "phrases of prepositions.")

Of course, some will inevitably creep in (even more inevitably in nonfiction). One of the biggest favors you can do for yourself during the revision process is spot-checking for prepositions. Spend an entire draft just looking for them. There are many, but the most common in fiction are "to" "in" "by" "for" and the most pervasive one: "of." Say "of" aloud a few times. What a yucky word. Who wants that in their manuscript? Take it out and replace it with a more powerful word. Your sentence will be shorter and clearer as a result. You'll streamline your writing by clearing away clutter, allowing your reader to focus on your story.

Does this mean you can never use a prepositional phrase? No. There may be a few that prove impossible to replace. But once you've expunged them from your manuscript, you can put one or two back without any damage. You may even be able to find a way to use the occasional prepositional phrase effectively.

Remember JFK's stirring inaugural address? Here's an excerpt:

> The torch has been passed to a new generation of Americans, born in this century, tempered by war,

disciplined by a hard and bitter peace, proud of our ancient heritage.

That's several prepositional phrases in a row. And still the passage works (though it's much better delivered by a fine orator like JFK than when read on the printed page). JFK (or perhaps his speechwriter, Ted Sorenson) used prepositional phrases skillfully and purposefully, employing the rhetorical device known as parallelism. Each succeeding clause follows a pattern, specifically, a verb (or in the last case, an adjective) followed by a prepositional phrase (in this century, by war, etc.). The result is syntactic symmetry. The lines acquire a cadence or rhythm. This is what makes the passage so memorable (especially when it's read aloud, since rhythm and cadence are sonic devices).

For the most part, writers don't compose novels with an eye on the audiobook. The largest part of your audience will read it silently. Your focus, therefore, should be on that reading experience. Streamline your sentences as much as possible, focusing on putting the right word in the right place—and eliminating the ones that just get in the way.

Highlights

1) The difference between the almost right word and the right word is the difference between the lightning bug and the lightning.

2) The fundamental structure of any English language sentence is subject-verb-object (if there is an object).

3) No word is unimportant. Every single one matters. So choose each one carefully.

4) Eliminate every word that does not convey meaning.

5) Avoid sentences beginning with "There were" or "This was" or "It was."

6) Eliminating prepositional phrases will streamline your prose.

Red Sneaker Exercises

1) Want to see the difference choosing the right word can make? Go to YouTube and watch the film titled "The Power of Words." See what happens when a clever person rewrites.

2) Time for another exercise in Find and Replace. This time, go through your manuscript and search for the word "of." After you recover from your horror, roll up your sleeves and see how many you can eliminate, either by removing preposition phrases or by removing phrasal

verbs. It probably won't take as long as you think. And even if it takes all day, the exercise will help concretize a new and better approach to writing in your brain.

3) Some words like "government" and "bailout" are supercharged with connotation. Words like that can be used skillfully by writers to create specific emotional responses, but written randomly or inadvertently can cause unexpected problems. You should particularly avoid words that have political resonance if you're not writing a political novel, because you're likely to alienate someone. Are there any supercharged words in your manuscript? Do you need them? Would it be better to eliminate them?

4) Do you have a proofreading plan in place? Something to prevent you from omitting important words or thoughts? Think of it as an insurance policy against problematic omissions like Neil Armstrong's "a." Your outside editors don't necessarily need to be writers or English majors. The only requirements are that they read, that they have a good feel for the language, and that they're not afraid to tell you what they really think. Hearing "Wow, Bill, that was terrific," may give me warm fuzzies, but it won't make my book any better. You need a reader who has the fortitude to provide useful input.

5) Review a few chapters from your manuscript at random. Do you see any recurring patterns? An overused way of expressing yourself? A tendency to start sentences the same way? If so, it's time to return to your old friend, Find and Replace. Rewrite those sentences to make them more dynamic, less static. Give your sentences true subjects, definite nouns, rather than pronouns. Rewriting is

hard work, but the effort will make your story more powerful.

CHAPTER 6: SPOTLIGHT ON VERBS

Respect the verbs in your life.
Life is a verb. Live is a verb.
Live Life. Action verbs
bring life to writing.
Love is a verb. Be is a verb.
Be in Love...

Jerriann Wayahowl Law

Verbs are arguably the most important part of any sentence, and never more so than when you're writing fiction. When your reader experiences your story, it should run, jump, sing, shout, and never seem to stand still. Even if you're writing the most introspective character-driven novel, the reader should have a sense of forward momentum. The narrative should push ahead, not run in place.

That's why verbs are so important. Verbs are supposed to lend action to your story, to make it come to life. Unfortunately, all too often, either due to laziness or bad habits, writers bury or suppress the action by picking weak verbs, or to-be verbs, or no verbs at all. This will not lead to absorbing storytelling. This will lead to a static narrative all too likely to be put down quickly by the reader.

WILLIAM BERNHARDT

Lights, Camera...Action!

First let's discuss the verbs you don't want in your fiction, then we'll move to the verbs you do want. I can put the verbs to avoid in three categories:

1) to-be verbs,
2) helping verbs (yes, there's overlap here), and
3) nominalizations.

Perhaps you're wondering why I have a problem with to-be verbs: is, are, was, were, am, be, become, and became. They are proper verbs, right? They are grammatically correct, aren't they? Yes, but you're a fiction writer, squarely in the descriptive school, so simply following rules is not enough. When you use to-be verbs, you impart no action to the sentence and thus no life to the story. All a to-be verb tells the reader is that something exists. It doesn't tell you anything about it, much less convey a sense of action. That's just not enough for fiction.

Although this is far from the only time to-be verbs crop up, aspiring writers tend to rely upon them most extensively when they're describing. Have you written passages like that? "The room was dark. The walls were green. There was no way out..." In my book on Description I'll suggest other more powerful and engaging approaches, but for now suffice to say that the best descriptions are integrated with the story.

Probably every writer on earth puts too many to-be verbs in their first draft. Don't despair. Just remember that you have a lot of work to do in the future. In time, you will probably find yourself rewriting in your head and instinctively shying away from to-be verbs in favor of more dynamic, high-energy verbs. One aspiring writer with whom I've worked devoted an entire draft to systematically

78

plowing through her manuscript and removing every "was." This was probably tedious work, but she later sold that book, and I'm betting she doesn't have to spend as much time doing that now as she did the first time.

Avoid to-be verbs: is, are, was, were, am, be, become, and became.

When used in conjunction with another verb, these words are sometimes called "helping verbs." They are actually no help at all, at least not to the fiction writer. Those helping verbs distance the reader from the action. They undercut the verbs to which they are attached and undermine their effectiveness.

Consider the following two constructions of the same idea:

She was reading the book.

She read the book.

Do you feel the difference? To me, it isn't even subtle. The helping verb "was" gets in between the subject and the real verb and distances the reader from the action. When you omit the helper (and switch to the past-tense form of the verb), you lose nothing in terms of meaning, but gain a great deal in terms of immediacy. In one of the most famous passages in the King James translation of the Bible, you don't read:

Jesus was weeping.

you read:

Jesus wept.

79

Both the brevity and the omission of the helping verb give the sentence power.

Avoid helping verbs.

Nominalizations (sometimes called "nounifications") are verbs that have been transformed into nouns, usually with a considerable loss of power and impact. The more powerful verb has been turned into a noun, leaving a weaker verb to take its place. You often see nominalizations in the business world, sometimes deliberately employed to defang the verb. But as a fiction writer, you want every word to pack as much punch as possible.

See the difference?

The parties engaged in litigation.

(The verb "litigate" has been turned into a noun and replaced by the vague, jargony verb "engaged").

The parties litigated.

(Let the verb be a verb and the sentence is more direct and powerful.)

The parties sued.

(Put the sentence in more common language and the sentence will be even more immediate.)

Try to stomp out nominalizations whenever possible. They suggest someone more interested in flaunting long words than generating any excitement. In the business world, that may be acceptable, but in fiction, it never is.

See if you can sense the difference in immediacy and impact in the following sentence pairs:

We are in agreement about this.
We agree.

The coroner performed an analysis of the blood.
The coroner analyzed the blood.

The king was of the opinion that the jester was lying.
The king thought the jester lied.

The lovers had an understanding.
The lovers understood.

I hope you see the difference. Eliminate those to-be verbs, helping verbs, and nominalizations, and you'll find yourself writing much more powerful sentences.
Avoid nominalizations.

Muscle Verbs

Since I've told you what verbs to avoid, and I previously suggested that you shy away from degree adverbs, you may be wondering what you're allowed to write. The answer is what I call "muscle verbs," meaning dynamic verbs, words that resonate with information and action.

Some verbs are simply better than others. Writing is a dangerous field in which to be asserting rules, but a strong verb usually does one or both of two things: it conveys strong, readily visualized action, and/or it creates a strong emotional or sensory resonance.

It's probably easier to provide examples than to chat about it:

81

> After the transformation of the noun phrases into action verbs, the text will contain fewer abstractions; similarly, readers' capacities for visualization of the activities in discussion will be amplified.

That hideous sentence contains all three of the verb errors I suggested you avoid, plus part is in passive voice (that's our next topic). What happens when you get rid of all that junk and substitute a few muscle verbs?

> Dynamic action verbs transform your writing into powerful sentences that are easier to visualize.

Better, right? And not just because it's shorter, though that certainly helps, as does the omission of the semicolon, a punctuation mark that might work in academic papers but has no place in fiction. (Make it two separate sentences already.)

Earlier we discussed the uselessness of degree adverbs. You're probably also aware that from Hemingway forward, most first-rate writers have stifled their use of all kinds of adverbs. Occasionally one may be justifiable, but all too often, the use of an adverb is a sign that the writer has chosen the wrong verb. In other words, they're channeling the lightning bug rather than the lightning.

If you showed me a manuscript with a sentence like, "The man walked slowly," my response would be, "Ditch the adverb." But wait, you might reply. I need that adverb to show that he was walking in a particular manner— slowly. Otherwise, the reader might think he was walking at a normal pace. "You're missing the point," I would respond. "Your problem is not that you need an adverb. It's that you chose the wrong verb."

Instead of using vague verbs, which tend to be the ones that first leap to mind, dig a little deeper and use a more specific, more descriptive verb.

Rather than saying:

The man walked slowly.

instead write:

The man strolled.

or:

The man ambled.

And if he's moving quickly, don't say he "walked quickly," say he "ran" or "raced" or "darted" or "sprinted." If he's a proud or heroic figure, perhaps he "strode." You've communicated critical information without overt telling, simply by choosing the right verb. These verbs are perfectly common and readily understood, but far more descriptive and more likely to create a vivid mental image in your reader's mind than adverbs.

Consider a few more paired sentences:

The bell rang.
The bell clanged.

The sludge dripped.
The sludge oozed.

The parasol moved in the wind.
The parasol swayed.

In these cases, the second sentence employs a stronger, more descriptive verb that also creates a sensory impression. Words like "clanged" and "oozed" touch on our five senses, which is the best way to bring a descriptive passage alive—much better than slavering on adverbs.

Strive for muscle verbs, specific descriptive action verbs that need no adverbs to create strong sensory impressions.

Passive Voice is to be Avoided

You probably recall an English teacher at some point in your life telling you to write in the active voice rather than the passive voice. Possibly you absorbed the rule but not the reason. Too often passive voice goes down like one of many grammatical rules that seem arbitrary and not terribly important. But this one is important. I'm giving the topic its own section because avoiding it will dramatically improve the quality of your writing. Like hyphenating phrasal adjectives and applying the Oxford comma, this is an example of a rule that is not a myth, but a rule that is indeed a rule and for good reason. Passive voice distances the reader from the action being described because it makes murky who did what.

This is not precisely a verb issue, but I've included it in this section because one of the flaws of passive voice— though not the only one—is that it almost inevitably results in the use of a to-be verb.

Are you clear on what passive voice is? The technical definition is: If the subject of a transitive verb does not perform the action, it's passive voice. Perhaps a simpler approach would be, if you can't tell who did what, it's passive voice. If the sentence seems to deliberately hide or delay stating who performed the action described by the verb, it's passive voice. If the sentence seems to leave an unanswered question—"By whom?"—it's passive voice. (Some teachers are now replacing the question "By whom?" with "By zombies?" Either way works.)

Consider this sentence:

The deadline was not met.

By whom? The sentence does not explain who failed to meet the deadline. Technically, the subject of the sentence is "deadline," but the deadline didn't perform any action. Hence, passive voice. Here's a better construction:

The reporter did not meet the deadline.

Now we know who performed the action (and it wasn't a zombie). The reporter is the subject, because she's the one who performed the action of the verb (failing). Deadline has been moved to the place of the object, as it should be, because it did not perform the action, it was acted upon.

Passive voice distances readers from the action and slows reading because you're not expressly saying who did what. Passive voice makes it harder for the reader to process information because you've inverted the natural word order of the English language sentence. The result is less immediate and less effective.

Passive voice is to be avoided. Which of course should be rewritten

You should avoid passive voice.

Isn't that better?

Is there ever a good reason to employ passive voice? In fiction, I doubt it, but in other realms, a reason may occasionally arise when you deliberately want to make the sentence more attenuated. Lawyers sometimes retreat to passive voice when speaking to the judge. Appeal briefs conclude with "Judgment should be affirmed," because it sounds more deferential and less in-your-face than, "You should affirm the judgment," which comes perilously close to telling the judge what to do, never a good idea. Passive voice is also sometimes used in academic and scientific papers. Sadly, sometimes I suspect insecure writers think passive voice makes them sound more sophisticated. "It is suggested by the ancient Greeks…" The reality is, passive voice sounds pompous and ineffectual.

You see passive voice crop up occasionally in the world of politics, usually when someone is deliberately trying to sever the connection between actor and action. At the end of the protracted Iran-Contra scandal, President Reagan finally appeared on national television and admitted that there had been an arms-for-hostages swap in contravention of congressional directives. But how did he admit this? Do you recall what has now become a famous quote? What did he actually say?

"Mistakes were made."

By whom, Mr President? (It wasn't zombies.) Reagan chose not to go there, a savvy choice, especially since Oliver North acknowledged that the President knew what was happening when it happened. Reagan wanted to admit the error without blaming anyone or admitting fault. So passive voice made sense. But I can't think of a time when a fiction writer wants to distance the reader from the story. So stick with active voice.

WILLIAM BERNHARDT

Highlights

1) Avoid to-be verbs: is, are, was, were, am, be, become, and became.

2) Avoid helping verbs.

3) Avoid nominalizations.

4) Strive for muscle verbs, specific descriptive action verbs that need no adverbs and create strong sensory impressions.

5) Avoid passive voice.

Red Sneaker Exercises

1) Bet you saw this exercise coming. Do another search and destroy mission with Find and Replace, this time looking for those to-be/helping verbs. Chances are you're writing in past tense so you're using "was" more frequently than the others. Can you reduce your usage to a minimum? Be prepared for this exercise to take awhile—but recognize that it's worth the effort.

2) Fiction is always improved by strong verbs that recreate specific sensory impressions, but this is particularly true in action scenes and descriptive passages. When your characters are fighting, running, or struggling, either physically or emotionally, strong muscle verbs will bring the scene to life much better than "telling" passages that feed the reader information about the characters' emotional

states. Descriptions that are integrated into the story, revealing the environment as your character experiences it, will be more powerful than a long series of "was" sentences. Find an action sequence or descriptive passage in your work and see if you can make it better.

3) Closely related to passive voice is the word "had," which similarly distances the reader from the action. "Had" is fine when you're indicating ownership, but not when you're using it as a helping verb. This can arise in many situations, but I see it most frequently when writers are filling in backstory, telling the reader what happened in the past. See if you can rewrite an expository scene without using "had."

CHAPTER 7: OTHER STYLE ISSUES

The style is the man himself.

George-Louis Leclerc de Buffon

This last chapter is a potpourri, a grab bag of style issues worthy of discussion that have not arisen in the previous chapters. You should also check Appendix A for other potential style issues you want to avoid.

The Big Bang Theory

Neurolinguistics is a fascinating field and anyone who aspires to be a writer could benefit from studying words and the impact they have on the human brain. But for this section, I will simply tell you about one of the most interesting and practical discoveries of neurolinguistics relating to "emphatic words." Some words, it seems, have greater impact on readers then others. In the English language, the words most likely to resonate, the words most likely to strike home with the reader, are the words that come at the end of a sentence. Therefore, a writer wants to put the most powerful part of the sentence, the big bang, at the end whenever possible.

The primary point of emphasis in any English language sentence is at the end.

Think of writing a book like composing a piece of music. You want a dramatic finale, right? So you want to end with a big crash of the cymbals, not some tiny tinkling on a triangle. You want the big crescendo, something that will move the audience and leave them breathless.

Fiction writing is much the same. You want each sentence to make its point, each paragraph to make an even stronger point, and each scene to have a powerful impact. So write your sentences accordingly. Some people call this backloading the sentence—saving for the end the part that is most likely to resonate.

Standup comics already know this. If you don't believe me, turn on Comedy Central and watch a standup comic work. The typical joke or one-liner can be broken down into distinct parts: the innocent transition, the setup, and the unexpected twist. It's that last part that produces the laugh, so of course the comic saves it for the end. Similarly, if you're using strong words, or delivering a big surprise or ironic twist—put it at the end.

Consider the following two constructions:

> She realized all her hopes and dreams were childish fantasies because she had not yet matured as a person.

> She realized that because she had not matured as a person, her hopes and dreams were childish fantasies.

Can you see (or hear) the difference made by putting the emphatic, knife-twisting, gut-wrenching part of the sentence at the end?

Your Mother Was Right

Perhaps at some time or another your mother told you it was rude to interrupt. She was right. It's also a bad idea to interrupt yourself. You can interrupt your own sentence in many different ways. You can do it by interjecting an additional thought with dashes, or commas, or semicolons, or parentheses—but it's almost always better if you don't.

I hope by now you're realizing that writing is hard— possibly harder than you realized. I don't say that to discourage you. Just the opposite. I say it to encourage you to work hard and keep trying. By this point, you should realize how easily a sentence can go astray and end up not communicating what you wanted it to communicate. So if you can actually write one good sentence that expresses one idea clearly and succinctly—-quit while you're ahead. Don't use punctuation to cram a second thought into the same sentence.

Don't interrupt the main idea of a sentence.

Dashes can sometimes be used to show haste or excitement, as discussed in my book on Dialogue. But using them to thrust a second idea into a sentence is rarely a good idea. You'll slow down the reader, so make sure whatever dramatic purpose you intend is worth it. Worse, you may cause reader confusion, temporary or permanent. And no dramatic device justifies that.

This is what you want to avoid:

Bridget needed to meet with the artists, who just moved up to the fifth floor, so they could explain how to mix paints.

You see how a second, largely irrelevant idea was thrust into the middle of the sentence? In most cases, this will cause the reader to backtrack. They start on the first idea, then suddenly are plunged into the second. When they hit the last part of the sentence, after the second comma, they have to go back to the start to remind themselves what it was about, then connect it to the end of the sentence, this time skipping the intrusive middle. It would've been much easier, and clearer, if you had written two separate sentences for the two different ideas. Or dropped the middle clause altogether, because it seems irrelevant and doesn't pertain to the central idea. Once again, prepositional phrases, or dependent and independent clauses, are more likely to unnecessarily complicate your sentence than to improve it.

The problem increases with the length and difficulty of the sentence:

Since she did not know how to distribute her income tax-free through a charitable trust, which can only be effectuated by a specialist attorney when there are both a valid charitable purpose and regular charitable disbursements, she decided to try something different.

Much simpler, and less intrusive, if you simply write:

Since she did not know how to distribute her income tax-free through a charitable trust, she decided to try something different.

Isn't that easier to follow? If you need to give your reader that additional information, put it in a separate sentence. But you may find that all that intrusive information, once deleted, is not much missed.

De-centuate the Negative

Whenever possible, make statements in the positive, rather than the negative.

This is a good rule of thumb for writers, and not simply because optimists are more pleasant to read than pessimists (though that is certainly true). Readers more readily absorb information stated in the positive (again, knowledge gained from neurolinguistics). Furthermore, stating the positive, what exists rather than what does not, generally allows you to use more powerful language. Too often, readers use many words to state the negative when they could more succinctly and vividly state the positive.

Compare these two possibilities:

Jonathan was not a very generous person.

Jonathan was a skinflint.

Or miser. Or tightwad. Choose the word you think is right given the tone and context of your sentence (because as Billy Collins has said, there's no such thing as a synonym). But the sentence will be tighter and more effective if you choose the right word—the lightning bolt—that describes what your character is, rather than using many words to describe what he is not.

Same thing here:

Bill is not a terribly coordinated guy.

Bill is a klutz.

or...

Marcia was not an even-tempered sober-minded woman.

Marcia was a shrew.

See the difference? Of course, it might be even better if you can show your reader what your character is like rather than telling them (see the book on Character).

Parallelism

Writing fiction can be challenging, because while you recognize that brevity is usually the best approach, you also want to write with vigor. You want variation in sentence length, sentence openers, and sentence structure. But you never want to lose the reader, so avoid writing unbalanced, or non-parallel sentences.

When a sentence has multiple parts, the individual parts should be parallel.

A sentence can have multiple parts because it contains a list, or because separate sentences or thoughts are connected with a conjunction, or because you've inserted a semicolon (though I hope it's not the latter. I hate semicolons).

Do you see a problem with this sentence?

Karen ordered all the section chiefs to pay greater attention to improving productivity, expense reduction, and addressing customer needs.

Even if you didn't immediately see the problem, did you get a nagging feeling that something wasn't quite right in that sentence? Your reader will get the same feeling—and that's why you want to avoid it.

The problem is that the sentence contains a list of three items to which the chiefs should pay attention, but the list is not parallel. Two of them are present participles ("improving" and "addressing") while the other is not. Even without knowing the grammatical term, though, you can see that two of the items contain -ing words and one does not. The result is a sentence that seems awkward and clunky.

A sentence reads much more smoothly when all the items in the list match one another grammatically:

> Karen ordered the section chiefs to pay greater attention to improving productivity, reducing expenses, and addressing customer needs.

Or alternately and more succinctly:

> Karen ordered the section chiefs to improve productivity, reduce expenses, and address customer needs.

Several years ago, the Harvard Business School ran an ad with this slogan:

> What's innovative, global, challenging, demanding, enlightening, and produces leaders?

William Safire called them out on it in one of his columns. You see the problem? The question presents a list of one-word adjectives—culminating in a verb-object combo. The result is awkward. I can see the source of Harvard's problem. I can't think of a good one-word adjective that means "produces leaders." But that's no excuse for a clumsy sentence, especially from such a prestigious institution.

Focus on Strong Sensory Words

In the discussion of verbs, I emphasized the value of strong verbs and verbs that trigger sensory impressions. Here I want to emphasize that this is always true, not just with verbs.

Get rid of weak, sluggish words.

Some of the words I try to avoid in fiction include: maybe, perhaps, noticed, wondered, thought, just, started, began, tried, guessed, like, well, some, sort of, nearly, realized, suddenly, and now.

Many of these words indicate weak or vague thinking. Some are overused. Some are thinly veiled degree adverbs. As discussed in Dialogue, conversational passages are rarely enhanced with words like "wondered" or "realized."

Most sentences become more immediate if you lose the "started to" or "began to" and just have your character perform the action. As a writer, you're initiating a new action, so this is a natural phrase to write, but for the reader, it will create a more effective image if you skip the warm-up and just have it happen. The same is true of "tried to" unless you're making the point that the character tried and failed to accomplish something.

"Suddenly" is often used by amateur writers to inject excitement into a book. It doesn't work. Instead describe something happening suddenly. Use your descriptive skills. Don't rely on adverbs to generate heat—they won't.

"Now" is usually a bad idea in a novel, if you're describing something as happening "now," because from the reader's standpoint, everything you describe is happening now, that is, everything happens as they read it. Using "now" seems redundant and in some cases, confusing.

It would be unfair of me to give you a list of words to avoid without also offering some words you can use. Here are a few examples of strong words that conjure sensory impressions: snooped, fragrant, musky, bitter, juicy, caressed, barren, brisk, licks, bellows, blood-soaked, howled, and chirped.

Do I need to explain why? In addition to describing what they describe, these words touch on the five senses and thus affect the reader emotionally. You won't need an additional adjective or adverb when you use these words. The best (such as "blood-soaked" or "bitter") touch upon more than one sense, making them even more powerful.

Make Your Writing Memorable

I can write on and on about writing style (in fact, I just did). But what's the one thing that will make your work more powerful than anything else?

Write something interesting. Unique. Emotional. Meaningful. Memorable.

I don't need to reiterate that you must seize your readers' attention. If you don't, you won't have it for long. In the Seventies, the term "information overload" was coined, but today, we have so much information thrown at us every day that the Seventies seem calm and rustic by comparison. On a typical business day, the average worker is exposed to more than three hundred marketing messages via radio, television, billboards, transit ads, office ads, email, etc. The advent of digital books and the Internet have created an almost endless wealth of reading material. Given this barrage of data, how do you get attention for your story?

By writing it well. By observing the lessons in the other books in this series, yes, so you have a good story. But then you must tell it exceptionally well. Tell it memorably, dramatically, and purposefully. Follow all the guidelines in this book and fuse them with your own creativity and your own unique voice. Tell the story you were meant to tell. Use every word to maximum effect, because every word matters.

Remember, every time you write you have the power to change the world. So do the best job you possibly can. Set the world on fire.

SIZZLING STYLE

Highlights

1) The primary point of emphasis in any English language sentence is at the end.

2) Don't interrupt the main idea of a sentence.

3) Whenever possible, make statements in the positive, rather that the negative.

4) When a sentence has multiple parts, the individual parts should be parallel.

5) Get rid of weak, sluggish words.

6) Write something interesting. Unique. Emotional. Meaningful. Memorable.

Red Sneaker Exercises

1) Do you have a tendency to overuse dashes (like me) or commas or semicolons or some other habit that makes sentences unnecessarily complex? If so, conduct a Find search for the offending habit, then explore different ways of living without it.

2) Start making a list of powerful, vivid, sensory words. Next time you read a sentence that strikes you as effective, take a moment to stop and consider why. Next time you find yourself absorbed in a story, your pulse pounding or your eyes resisting sleep, take a moment to consider why.

WILLIAM BERNHARDT

What is that writer doing right? What style tips could you learn and apply to your own work?

3) Consider your goal for this book. What are you trying to achieve (and no vague responses like "getting published" or "making money"). What impact would you like to have on your readers? Once you've got that figured out, look back over this book and consider how you will use language, the most powerful tool we possess, to accomplish your goal.

APPENDIX A: STYLE REVIEW

1) Avoid weak openings, such as "Pronoun Followed by To-Be Verb," as in, "It is" and "There are" and "They are." Instead, use definite subjects and strong action verbs that bring energy and precision to your sentence. You can often fix sentences that start this way by inverting them, that is, by converting the object into the subject.

2) Avoid to-be verbs whenever possible. Instead of using them as helping verbs, change the tense of the verb and ditch the helper.

3) Eliminate unnecessary words. The longer the sentence, the more difficult it is for a reader to absorb. Many words before the subject, or between the subject and the verb, or between the verb and the object, will make the sentence more difficult to follow.

4) Work to find the precise word to say exactly what you want to say in the strongest possible way.

5) Eliminate redundancy.

6) Avoid word repetition, particularly words repeating in the same sentence or paragraph.

7) Eliminate embarrassing grammar errors such as subject-verb agreement problems. If you're unsure about a rule, look it up.

8) Avoid clichés. Invent fresh and original ways of expressing your thoughts.

9) Don't risk misspellings that erode confidence. Use a dictionary app to your advantage.

10) If you're tempted to use an adverb, try choosing a stronger verb instead. Avoid all degree adverbs, such as "very" and "really" and "pretty."
11) Use the Oxford comma.
12) The titles of short works should be put in quotation marks. The titles of long works should be italicized.
13) Punctuation marks should be placed inside the quotation marks.
14) Don't use "snicker quotes," that is, don't use quotation marks to mean "so-called."
15) Avoid prepositional phrases and other unnecessary words that clutter and complicate your sentences.
16) If a word doesn't contribute anything to your sentence, take it out.
17) Multiple-word (phrasal) adjectives should be hyphenated, as in "multiple-word adjectives."
18) Avoid passive voice, unless you're using it for a specific strategic reason. Active voice will give your sentences more immediacy and power.
19) Write out numbers whenever practical.
20) Do many drafts of everything you write, and somewhere toward the end of the revision process, consider reading your work aloud. You may catch typos and other embarrassing errors you miss when reading silently.

APPENDIX B: COMMONLY CONFUSED WORDS

Affect/Effect: Contrary to the commonly espoused rule, both words can be used as nouns and verbs, depending upon your meaning. *Affect* is usually a verb meaning "to have an effect on," but it can also be used to mean "countenance" or "emotion," as in, "The Vulcan had a flat affect." *Effect* is usually a noun meaning "impact" or "consequence," but it can also be used as a verb (a shortened form of "effectuate") meaning "to bring about."

Aggravate/Irritate: *Aggravate* means to worsen. *Irritate* means to inflame or anger. Many people use *aggravate* to mean "vex, annoy, or irritate," but that is not strictly speaking correct.

Allude/Refer: Yes, there is a difference. To *allude* is "to hint at or mention indirectly." To *refer* is "to mention directly." "Are you alluding to my height when you call me 'Napoleon?'" "You're short," she said, referring to his height.

Alternate/Alternative: *Alternate* means "one after the other." *Alternative* means "one instead of the other." Walking requires the *alternate* use of the left and right foot. The *alternative* is the bus.

Amused/Bemused: *Amused* means you're having a good time. *Bemused* means you're befuddled or puzzled or deep in thought.

Attorney General/Attorneys General: The plural of *attorney general* is *attorneys general,* as in: "Several assistant attorneys general appeared on behalf of the state." In this phrase, *general* is an adjective following the noun (a postpositive adjective), not a noun. The same is true of "Presidents Elect" or "mothers-in-law" or "passersby," but is not correct for a true compound word such as "spoonful." The plural would be "spoonfuls," not "spoonsful."

Besides/Beside: *Besides* means other than or in addition. *Beside* means alongside. "No one *besides* her son could stand so close beside her."

Big of a/Big of: As always, eliminate unnecessary words that add nothing to the sentence. Don't say, "How *big of a* case is it?" The same is true of "long of a" "slow of a" and other similar constructions.

Childlike/Childish: *Childish* is a pejorative adjective suggesting that someone is acting like a child and that isn't good. The positive way of saying the exact same thing is *childlike.*

Complement/Compliment: To *complement* is to complete or pair with or round out. To *compliment* is to praise.

Continuous/Continual: *Continuous* means uninterrupted.

Continual means repeated, but intermittent. "Jack had to wind the grandfather clock continually to make it run continuously."

Convince/Persuade: You *convince* someone of something, but you *persuade* them to do something. *Convince* is usually followed by "that" or "of," but *persuade* is always followed by "to."

Corroborate/Collaborate: To *corroborate* evidence is to fortify it with additional evidence. To *collaborate* on a project is to work with someone else on it.

Could/Couldn't Care Less: If your intent is to say that you care as little as it is possible to care, use the phrase "couldn't care less." If you could care less, that means you already care at least a little.

Counsel/Council: *Counsel* means "advice," but it can also be a noun meaning "lawyer" or "consultant," in effect, a shortened form of "counselor." *Council* is a committee that leads or governs.

Credulous/Incredible: The *incredible* is unbelievable. Credulous people are gullible. *Incredulous* means you do not believe.

Datum/Data: *Datum* is the traditional singular, *data* the plural, but today, many people use *data* as a singular noun and few dictionaries or grammarians are still suggesting that it is incorrect.

Deserts/Desserts: In this example: What one deserves is one's *just deserts*. This use of *deserts* is related to the verb *deserve*. "The unsuccessful plaintiff got his just deserts." Deserts are dry, arid, sandy places, preferably in Cabo, and desserts include tiramisu and sopaipillas.

Discreet/Discrete: *Discreet* means "careful" or "prudent." *Discrete* means "separate, distinct, or unconnected." "Jack was *discreet* about his secret for maintaining two wives and two *discrete* households."

Disinterested/Uninterested: *Disinterested* means impartial or fair. *Uninterested* means not interested, bored, unengaged. "The judge was disinterested in the outcome of the case, and uninterested in the uncivil behavior of the divorce attorney."

Divorcé/Divorcée: *Divorcé* is for men, *divorcée* is for women.

Elicit/Illicit: To *elicit* is to evoke. *Illicit* means "illegal."

Emigrate/Immigrate: It's all about coming and going. You *emigrate* from a country and *immigrate* to another. For a mnemonic, remember that "exit" starts with an "e," like "*emigrate*," and "in" starts with an "i," like "*immigrate*."

Eminent/Imminent/Immanent: *Eminent* means "famous or superior." *Imminent* means "impending." *Immanent* (rare these days, outside of the church) means "inherent or dwelling within."

SIZZLING STYLE

Farther/Further: *Farther* refers to physical distance. *Further* means "to a greater extent or degree."

Fewer/Less: "Fewer" is used when the items in question can be counted. "Less" is used for items not subject to easy enumeration. "We had *fewer* writers than we'd hoped for, but *less* optimism than I expected." Obviously, the sign in every supermarket reading "Ten Items or Less" is just wrong.

Hadn't/Hadn't of: "*Hadn't of*" is ugly and grammatically incorrect.

Hanged/Hung: Murderers and horse thieves used to be *hanged*. "Hung" is incorrect in that context. But paintings and coats are *hung*.

Historic/Historical: *Historic* means "having a place in history." *Historical* means "pertaining to the subject of history."

Home in/Hone in: "We need to *home* in on the precise problem."

Imply/Infer: To imply means to suggest something. To infer means to conclude from available evidence. Speakers imply. Listeners infer. Writers imply. Readers infer. "You imply that I'm a moron," the husband said. "You infer correctly," the wife replied.

Ingenuous/Ingenious: *Ingenuous* means naïve, frank, or candid, coming from the same root word as "ingénue."

Ingenious means crafty. Disingenuous means dishonest.

It's/Its: *It's* is the contraction for *it is*. *Its* is a possessive pronoun.

Jones's/Joneses: One guy is a *Jones*, but the whole family are the *Joneses*. If you are discussing something they own, that would be the *Joneses'*. The same is true of other family names ending in "s."

Laudable/Laudatory: *Laudable* means praiseworthy. *Laudatory* means praiseful. "He did a laudable job of reading the laudatory psalms."

Lie/Lay: *Lie* means to recline. The simple past tense of *lie* is *lay* and the past participle is *lain*. Lay can also be a verb indicating placement, and therein lies the confusion. The past tense of *lay* is *laid*. "Today you *lie* in the same bed where I lay my car keys."

Memoranda/Memorandum: *Memoranda* is plural, *memorandum* is singular.

Neither/Nor: Whether the verb in a "neither/nor" sentence is singular or plural depends upon the second element. Therefore, "Neither you nor I *am* responsible," but, "Neither I nor they *are* responsible." "Neither" by itself means by implication "neither one," so it takes a singular verb, as in, "Neither of your objections *is* correct." The same is true for "either," as in: "Either the plaintiff or one of the other lawyers *is* responsible for the judge's verdict."

Number/Amounts: Countable items have a *number*. Non-countable items are measured in *amounts*.

Overflowed/Overflow: *Overflowed* is the past tense and past participle of the verb *overflow*.

Persecute/Prosecute: To *persecute* is to torment. To *prosecute* is to conduct criminal proceedings. "The defendant felt *persecuted* when the DA *prosecuted* him the second time."

Principal/Principle: *Principal* means "main or primary." *Principle* means "rule or standard." "The school principal said his principal goal was to reinvest the trust fund principal, as a matter of principle."

Prophesy/Prophecy: *Prophesy* is a verb meaning "to foretell." *Prophecy* is a noun indicating what was foretold. "Madame Martel dropped her fee per prophecy, because she could prophesy a downturn in the economy."

Prospective/Perspective: *Prospective* means "potential." *Perspective* means "viewpoint."

Ravage/Ravish: A famous headline in a Minnesota newspaper read: "Queen Elizabeth Ravished." As you might have guessed, the ocean liner *Queen Elizabeth* caught fire and burned, and the paper should have said "Queen Elizabeth Ravaged" (though that sill doesn't sound very good). *Ravaged* means "damaged or destroyed." *Ravished* means "carried away (by force or by emotion) or sexually assaulted." When you say that your sweetheart looked *ravishing*, you're not implying a desire to do anything illegal. You're saying the sight of her swept you away with emotion.

Regardless/Irregardless: *Irregardless* is still considered substandard by most authorities, though it technically has the same meaning as "regardless."

Regretful/Regrettable: *Regretful* means "full of regret." *Regrettable* means "unfortunate, a cause for regret." "Florence *regretfully* swept up the pieces of the Ming vase she had *regrettably* smashed."

Reigned/Reined: "The legal fees when Queen Elizabeth reigned had to be *reined* in by the Privy Council."

Reluctant/Reticent: Although people often use these as synonyms, their true meanings aren't even similar. *Reluctant* means unwilling, but *reticent* means silent. "The *reluctant* witness was *reticent* on the witness stand."

Stationer/Stationery/Stationary: A *stationer* sells *stationery* (a good mnemonic device is to recall that there is an *"er"* in *"paper"*). *Stationary* objects (like stationery) do not move.

Stolen/Robbed: Money and other things of value are *stolen*. People, places, and businesses are *robbed*.

Therefore/Therefor: *Therefore* means "accordingly" or "in conclusion." *Therefor* is an ugly and archaic piece of legalese meaning "for it" or "for them," as in, "He bought a bicycle and paid *therefor*."

Tortuous/Torturous: *Tortuous* means "winding or crooked or twisty." *Torturous* means "painful." "During the tortuous drive, Jack developed a torturous ache in his backside."

Who/Whom: Most modern grammarians now say "who" can always be used in place of "whom" at the beginning of a sentence or clause. "Whom" should still be used after a preposition. So "Who from?" is correct, but so is "From whom?" Most American lexicographers, from Daniel Webster on down, have argued for clarifying the confusion by eliminating "whom" altogether, but it hasn't happened yet.

Whose/Who's: *Whose* is the possessive relative pronoun. *Who's* is the contraction for *who is*. "*Who's* the person for *whose* benefit the trust fund was established?"

APPENDIX C: THE WRITER'S READING LIST

The Chicago Manual of Style. 16th ed. Chicago: University of Chicago Press, 2010.

Cook, Vivian. *All in a Word: 100 Delightful Excursions into the Uses and Abuses of Words.* Brooklyn: Melville House, 2010.

Fowler, H.W. *Fowler's Modern English Usage.* 3rd ed. Rev. Ernest Gowers. N.Y. & Oxford: Oxford University Press, 2004.

Goldman, William. *Adventures in the Screen Trade: A Personal View of Hollywood and Screenwriting.* New York: Grand Central, 1989.

Hale, Constance. *Sin and Syntax: How to Create Wickedly Effective Prose.* New York: Broadway Books, 2001.

Hart, Jack. *A Writer's Coach: The Complete Guide to Writing Strategies That Work.* New York: Anchor Books, 2006.

Jones, Catherine Ann. *The Way of Story: The Craft and Soul of Writing.* Studio City: Michael Wiese Productions, 2007.

WILLIAM BERNHARDT

Klauser, Henriette Anne. *Writing on Both Sides of the Brain.* San Francisco: Harper & Row, 1987.

Maass, Donald. *The Fire in Fiction: Passion, Purpose, and Techniques to Make Your Novel Great.* Cincinnati: Writers Digest Books, 2009.

Maass, Donald. *Writing the Breakout Novel: Insider Advice for Taking Your Fiction to the Next Level.* Cincinnati: Writers Digest Books, 2001.

Maass, Donald. *Writing 21st Century Fiction: High Impact Techniques for Exceptional Storytelling.* Cincinnati: Writers Digest Books, 2012.

O'Conner, Patricia T. *Woe Is I: The Grammarphobe's Guide to Better English in Plain English.* 2nd ed. New York: Riverhead Books, 2003.

O'Conner, Patricia T. *Origins of the Specious: Myths and Misconceptions of the English Language.* New York: Random House, 2009.

Strunk, William, Jr., and White, E.B. *The Elements of Style.* 4th ed. N.Y.: Macmillan, 2000.

Truss, Lynne. *Eats Shoots & Leaves: The Zero Tolerance Guide to Punctuation.* New York: Gotham Books, 2005.

Vogler, Christopher. *The Writer's Journey: Mythic Structure for Storytellers and Screenwriters.* Studio City: Michael Wiese Productions, 1992.

SIZZLING STYLE

Zinsler, William. *On Writing Well: The Classic Guide to Writing Nonfiction.* 30th Anniv. Ed. New York: Harper Perennial, 2006.

About the Author

William Bernhardt is the bestselling author of more than thirty books, including the blockbuster Ben Kincaid series of novels. In addition, Bernhardt founded the Red Sneaker Writing Center in 2005, hosting writing workshops and small-group seminars and becoming one of the most in-demand writing instructors in the nation. His programs have educated many authors now published at major New York houses. He holds a Masters Degree in English Literature and is the only writer to have received the Southern Writers Guild's Gold Medal Award, the Royden B. Davis Distinguished Author Award (University of Pennsylvania) and the H. Louise Cobb Distinguished Author Award (Oklahoma State), which is given "in recognition of an outstanding body of work that has profoundly influenced the way in which we understand ourselves and American society at large." In addition to the novels, he has written plays, including a musical (book and music), humor, nonfiction books, children's books, biography, poetry, and crossword puzzles. He is a member of the Author's Guild, PEN International and the American Academy of Poets.

CPSIA information can be obtained at www.ICGtesting.com
Printed in the USA
LVOW07s1452280915

456017LV00001B/56/P